Henry Barton Dawson

Major-General Israel Putnam

A Correspondence

Henry Barton Dawson

Major-General Israel Putnam
A Correspondence

ISBN/EAN: 9783744761628

Printed in Europe, USA, Canada, Australia, Japan

Cover: Foto ©ninafisch / pixelio.de

More available books at **www.hansebooks.com**

MAJOR-GENERAL ISRAEL PUTNAM.

A Correspondence, on this Subject,

WITH THE

EDITOR OF "THE HARTFORD DAILY POST,"

BY "SELAH," OF THAT CITY,

AND

HENRY B. DAWSON, OF WHITE PLAINS, N. Y.

MORRISANIA:

1860.

TO

GEORGE HENRY MOORE, ESQ.,

LIBRARIAN OF THE NEW YORK HISTORICAL SOCIETY,

AND

Author of "The Treason of Major-General Charles Lee,"

ONE OF THE FEW WHOSE VENERATION FOR "ESTABLISHED REPUTATIONS" DOES NOT

OVERCOME HIS FIDELITY AS A HISTORIAN,

AS A MEMENTO OF RESPECT

FOR HIS OWN ICONOCLASTIC LABORS,

AND OF

REGARD FOR HIM, AS AN EARLY AND CONSTANT FRIEND,

This Little Volume is Inscribed,

BY THE EDITOR.

MORRISANIA, N. Y., *September* 1, 1859.

INTRODUCTORY REMARKS.

During the past year, while engaged in the preparation of that portion of "*The Battles of the United States*" which relates, particularly, to the War of the Revolution, my attention was, necessarily, drawn to General Israel Putnam, of Connecticut, and to the part which he performed in that protracted struggle. On Noddle's Island, on Bunker's Hill, on the heights of Gowanus, and in the Highlands of the Hudson, it had been said, this officer had displayed great courage and extraordinary abilities: and these reports, added to the stories of his attack on the she-wolf, of his exploits in the old French War, of his courage in sitting on a barrel of onion-seed, of his ride down the bank at Horse-Neck, and of other feats, equally wonderful and no less fabulous, had made his name a "household word," which was synonymous with desperate courage, undeviating patriotism, and unquestioned integrity. An examination of the cotemporary documents, however, soon dispelled any illusion under which I may have labored before that time; and I satisfied myself that, if an example was required for the imitation of my countrymen, either in courage, integrity, or patriotism, the very last who could be taken from among the officers of the Revolutionary Armies, for that purpose, would be General Israel Putnam.

[In my examination of the affairs on Noddle's Island and on Breed's Hill, I said but little on the subject; but in my account of "The Battle of Long Island" ("*Battles of the United States*," Book I, Chap. xi, Vol. I, pp. 143-150), I devoted more space to this subject, from the fact that, in that case, General Putnam was, actually, *the responsible commander*. After describing, as fully as I was capable, the several movements in that series of disasters, I closed the narrative with these words:

"The loss of the field, on Long Island, produced serious results in the American army. Nearly twelve hundred of the flower of the army were lost, a thousand of them being prisoners, among whom were Generals Sullivan and Lord Stirling. This defeat also discouraged the inexperienced troops under General Washington, and crowds of them left the army, spreading tales of terror wherever they went throughout the country, and working mischief, of the severest character, where its effect was most disastrous to the cause of America.

"There has been much comment on this battle, both respecting the action itself and those on whom the responsibility of the loss should fall. It has been well said, by one whose means of judging were unusually fine, that 'The strange oversight in leaving the Jamaica Road unguarded, and the neglect in procuring early and constant intelligence of the movements of the British army, were the immediate causes of the deplorable events of the day.' That there should be any doubt respecting the proper person to whom the loss of the battle of Long Island should be attributed, with these undisputed facts in view, is a matter of surprise to me. It is unquestionably the duty of the commander of a district to provide, not only the means of securing intelligence of every movement of his enemy, but for the protection of his position ; and, especially when any peculiar pass, or hill, or bridge, between him and the enemy, would secure advantages to that enemy, which would be dangerous to him, it is the unquestionable duty of the commander to occupy such position in force ; or, in case he neglects it, the disgrace is *his*, and the responsibility for any evil effects arising from such neglect of duty devolves upon *him*. In fact, the commander is a sentinel whom the commander-in-chief or the government has placed to guard the interests of the people; and, like any other sentinel, he cannot sleep on his post without committing one of the highest crimes known to the military law.

"With these axioms before us, let us examine, as far as the evidence goes, who commanded, and who slept on his post. It is said that General GREENE commanded on Long Island, that the defenses were thrown up under his direction, and that he was taken sick with a fever and left the island. It is said that General SULLIVAN then assumed the command; that, notwithstanding the enemy was still on Staten Island, he employed mounted patrols, at an expense of fifty dollars per night, to mount guard on roads which he saw the enemy might use in approaching New York ; and that, on the twenty-third of August—the day after the enemy's army landed on Long Island—he was superseded by General PUTNAM. It is said, and has never been contradicted, that General WASHINGTON gave General PUTNAM positive instructions to guard the passes through the hills leading to Brooklyn ; it is said, also without contradiction, that General SULLIVAN, his predecessor and second in command, enforced the same measures on his attention ; it is known, that, although the enemy, in full force, was encamped within four or five miles, opposite two of those very passes, General Putnam never reconnoitered that enemy's position—in fact, that he never left Brooklyn; and it is equally well known that, although the enemy was then encamped at Flatbush, the mounted patrols which General Sullivan had established, as well as the guards at some of the passes established by General Greene, were withdrawn, leaving the country clear for the enemy's secret movements, and the passes conveniently unguarded for his especial accommodation. It is also a well-established fact, that no general officer was outside the lines at Brooklyn, on the night of the twenty-sixth, until the advance of General Grant was made known to General Putnam, at three o'clock, when Generals Sullivan and Lord Stirling were dispatched to Flatbush and the Bay Road, to oppose the movements in those quarters.

"From these facts, it appears conclusively that General Putnam paid no attention to the orders of General Washington, respecting the security of the passes; and that the advice of General Sullivan, on the same subject, was also disregarded, his patrols withdrawn, and the command outside the lines, where his knowledge of the ground rendered him peculiarly useful, taken from him and given to another; that, with an enemy encamped in full force within a few miles of his position, he quietly remained at Brooklyn without reconnoitering that enemy's position, or sending out a scout; that he withdrew guards and failed to remount them, where they were essential to the safety of his position; and, finally, that to his ignorant, self-conceited inefficiency, the enemy is indebted for one of the greatest victories of the war, and his country for one of the most disastrous defeats, both military and moral, which it ever experienced.

"Yet, in the words of a modern writer, 'Not in vain was even the *defeat* of Brooklyn; not in vain, the anguish with which the usually calm spirit of Washington was that day torn. Not in vain were those two anxious days and nights which he passed on horseback, and which saved from death or captivity nine thousand men. These, and more, were all needed. In the immortal letters and dispatches of the great commander, and in the painful annals of the time, we read the cost and the value of what we are now enjoying. Without these we had not fully known how inherent, how enduring and elastic, is the power of an earnest and virtuous patriotism. Without them, even the transcendent name of Washington could not have filled the mighty measure of his fame.'"

In accordance with the plan of the work, I appended to this chapter the official reports of the several commanding officers and a short biographical sketch of General Putnam's life, the latter of which, from its connexion with the subject matter of this volume, I copy. It is embraced in these words:

"Israel Putnam was born at Salem, Massachusetts, on the seventh of January, 1718. Delighting more in the cultivation of those physical qualities which enabled him to surpass in feats of strength and agility, his mind was never cultivated, and he entered manhood without that solid practical information which, even at that early day, was within the reach of every New Englander. At the age of twenty-one he removed to Pomfret, Connecticut, where he engaged in the cultivation of a considerable tract of ground, which he had purchased. It was at this place that the tremendous "she-wolf," of which the world has heard so much, killed, it is said, *in one night*, seventy-five sheep and goats of his flock, besides wounding many of his lambs and kids; and there also is the wonderful cave where this terrible beast found refuge, and in which Mr. Putnam so gallantly confronted and killed her.

"When the French war broke out, he took the command of a company in Colonel Lyman's regiment of provincials; and, with it, joined the army near Crown Point. In the following year he rejoined the army, and it was in this campaign, while out on a scout near Ticonderoga, that the miraculous escape, so much spoken of and so well known, occurred: the *folded* blanket which he carried on his back, *when opened*, showing no less than fourteen bullet holes through it. In this campaign he appears also to have been taken prisoner by the Indians and carried to Montreal, from which he was exchanged through the assistance of Colonel Schuyler.

"After the peace he returned to his farm, where he remained until the troublesome times at Lexington and Concord aroused the country, and all New England seized their guns for the redress of their grievances. When 'the news from Lexington' reached Pomfret, Colonel Putnam was ploughing; and, it is said, he unyoked his team, mounted his horse, and hurried off to Cambridge. The General Assembly immediately afterwards authorized the organization of six regiments of troops, and Colonel Putnam (who had been appointed a Lieutenant-colonel of militia in October, 1774) was appointed to the command of the Third, with the title of Second Brigadier-general of the Provincial Troops. He speedily filled up his regiment, and returned at its head to Cambridge; a detachment from it, under the noble Captain Knowlton, having been among the troops ordered to Breed's Hill under Colonel Prescott, and whose cup of honest renown was filled to overflowing by their undaunted bravery on the eventful seventeenth of June.

"In a previous chapter, notice has been taken of the affair on Noddle's Island, and of the part which General PUTNAM did *not* take in it. It was his good fortune, however, to obtain the credit of that affair; and, through the management of interested parties in Congress, whose opposition to the commander-in-chief was then in embryo, but not less virulent, this intelligence, then just received in Congress, was so used as to secure for him the appointment of Major-general of the Continental Army, in June, 1775, to the mortification of General WASHINGTON, and the disgust of the officers from Massachusetts and Connecticut.

"At the battle of Bunker's Hill, he is said, by his eulogists, to have performed prodigies of valor. Those who were present, admit that he went on the ground with Colonel PRESCOTT and his party, on the evening before the battle, but they agree that he did not remain there. They say he returned on the following morning; but they agree that he ordered the intrenching tools to be removed from the redoubt, in opposition to the remonstrances of Colonel PRESCOTT, and for that purpose withdrew a large number of Colonel PRESCOTT's troops from the redoubt, at a time when the approach of the enemy showed that they were actually needed in the works. When the reinforcements under Colonel STARK came on the hill, they saw General PUTNAM and a large body of men quietly standing on the safe side of Bunker's Hill, beyond the range of the enemy's artillery; and when the same body retreated, after the struggle at the works was ended, the General and his men were at the same place, and quietly joined in the retreat. For his '*gallantry*' at Bunker's Hill, Colonel PRESCOTT—the acknowledged hero of that engagement—some years afterwards, at an official dinner with Governor BOWDOIN, of Massachusetts, openly declared General PUTNAM *deserved to be shot;* but those who were *not* there, and whose information is generally acquired from *less* reliable sources, generally suppose the venerable Colonel was mistaken in his conclusions, notwithstanding Colonel GERRISH, in whose company the General was, for *this very offense* (?), was afterwards *arrested for cowardice, tried by a court-martial, cashiered,* and *universally execrated.*

"On the reorganization of the army, under General WASHINGTON, General PUTNAM was ordered to the 'reserve' of the army. After the evacuation of Boston had relieved the colonies, for a season, of the presence of the enemy, General PUTNAM was sent forward to New York, to take the command there, and to continue the execution of the plan proposed by General LEE for the defense of that city, unless the general voice of the brigadiers and the engineers concurred in any *slight* change.

"After General WASHINGTON assumed the command in New York, General PUTNAM remained there, without command, until the sickness of General GREENE afforded an opportunity for the display of any abilities he might possess in opposing the enemy's progress towards New York. Of the manner in which he discharged his duty in that important position, this chapter has furnished some evidence.

"After the retreat into the county of Westchester, and the battle on Chatterton's Hill, General PUTNAM was ordered to Philadelphia; and in January, 1777, he was ordered to Princeton, where he remained until spring.

"In the spring of 1777, General PUTNAM was ordered to another of those quiet posts, where no particuliar abilities, beyond a strict obedience to orders, appeared to be required,—the command of the Highlands on the Hudson; but here, too, misfortunes visited him. After withdrawing the troops under his command beyond the limits within which they could render any assistance to the garrisons of Forts Montgomery and Clinton, leaving the passes exposed, and without even a guard or a patrol—in direct violation of the orders of the commander-in-chief—Sir HENRY CLINTON, as he had done at Bedford, on the twenty-seventh of August, stole a march on the vigilant and talented PUTNAM, and carried off the prizes, which furnished the key to the Highlands.

"In November, 1777, the situation of affairs in Pennsylvania rendered it necessary for General WASHINGTON to strengthen the army in that quarter. He accordingly dispatched Colonel HAMILTON, with orders to General PUTNAM, then at New Windsor, to send forward the brigades of Continental troops under Generals POOR and SULLIVAN, and the brigade of militia under General WARNER, to headquarters. But General PUTNAM had a desire to capture New York, and the commander-in-chief's orders were disregarded, until a letter, such as General WASHINGTON seldom wrote, brought the General to his senses. The result of this delay was the fall of Fort Mifflin, the evacuation of Red Bank, the loss of the defenses on the Delaware, and the continued occupation of Philadelphia, through the succeeding winter, by General HOWE.

"In March, 1778, Congress ordered an investigation of the causes which led to the loss of the forts in the Highlands, and General PUTNAM was superseded in his command by General McDOUGAL. The court of inquiry reported that, 'upon full knowledge and mature deliberation of facts, on the spot, they reported the loss to have been occasioned by *want of men, and not by any fault in the commanders.*' This indirect condemnation of the conduct of General PUTNAM, whose force had enabled him to supply the requisite number of men for the defense of the forts, was more positively confirmed by the action of General WASHINGTON, who ordered General PUTNAM to Connecticut, to 'superintend the forwarding on of the new levies,'—a post of far less importance than such a soldier as General PUTNAM is said to have been would have been placed in, at that important period, if those who knew the man, and who were fully competent to judge of his merits, had agreed with the popular opinion at the present day.

"It was during the General's residence in Connecticut that the celebrated descent down the slope at Horse-Neck (now Greenwich) took place. It is proper to state, however, that historians, or rather eulogists, have done the General great injustice respecting this affair. The steep was not quite *perpendicular*, as some have supposed; nor did his horse dash down the hill, as picture-makers have taken for granted, but, General PUTNAM himself being the witness, 'the horse was well trained and sagacious, and came down the hill in a sliding manner, resting upon his haunches,' the General, meanwhile, being almost as comfortable as when in his easy-chair by his fireside.

"General PUTNAM never afterwards enjoyed a separate command; and in 1779 he was rendered incapable of active duty of any kind, by an attack of paralysis, which, to a considerable extent, deprived him of the use of his limbs on one side.

"The remainder of his days were spent in retirement, and on the twenty-ninth of May, 1790, he died, aged seventy-two years."

In the preparation of these parts of my work, as in all others, I consulted nobody's taste or views but my own. My name was before the public as the author of the work; and, in this case, as in all others, *the exact truth, as I understood it,* was the only subject which I considered. I had written the pages which preceded these, with the single object of making a series of narratives which would stand the test of a thoroughly critical examination; and had known, *unjustly,* neither individual, nor party, nor country, in their preparation. Unknown beyond the immediate neighborhood in which I have lived and done business, from my boyhood, I was cheered onward, in this first attempt at book-making, by the words of approbation which I received from every quarter of the Union, and by the substantial evidences of confidence and respect which were voluntarily tendered and forwarded to me by the most honored of those who have added most honor to our Historic Literature, and I had seen no reason—nor have I yet seen any—to change the great fundamental principle on which I acted. I made as thorough an examination of my subject as my means would admit; and, after satisfying my own mind, with the same disregard of popular delusion and of professional chicanery which I have showed in all other parts of my work, I wrote and issued the lines which have been cited. I *presented* ISRAEL PUTNAM *as I found him*, as I have endeavored to do in the case of every other officer who occupied posts of similar importance ; and if General PUTNAM does not occupy the same relative position in my work, which others have assigned to him, *the fault, or the misfortune, was General* PUTNAM's, *not mine*.

The former of the two citations, involving the duties and responsibilities of a commander, soon after it appeared in print, was submitted, especially, to the critical examination of one of the most distinguished soldiers of our country, who has honored me with his friendship, and it met his full and unqualified approval. Sustained, as it has been, by the great weight of this authority, I have yet to learn that my conclusions are incorrect, or that in this, or in other parts of my work, I have exceeded my duty, as an humble laborer in the literature of our country.

About the time when the approval of my friend confirmed my own views on this subject, *the first and only attack which has been made on my work*, so far as I am aware, appeared, anonymously, in "*The Hartford Daily Post*," a widely circulating daily, which is published at Hartford, Connecticut. Through the kindness of some unknown friend, a copy of the paper which contained it was forwarded to me ; and, in consideration of *the personalities* which the article contained, I determined to offer a reply. The respected publisher, J. M. SCOFIELD, Esq., readily allowed me a hearing ; and I attempted to avail myself of the privilege in a respectful and dignified manner. A short time afterwards, my anonymous opponent, in a strain of personal abuse, renewed the attack ; and a second hearing was asked for, obtained, and employed in reply. Without being contented with his former efforts, my opponent, after some delay, appeared a third time—in which he received the co-operation of "an older, if not a better, soldier ;" and, a third time, I was subjected to the misrepresentation and abuse of "*Selah.*" With a degree of forbearance which entitles him to my grateful acknowledgments, Mr. SCOFIELD, a third time, opened his columns, for my answer—appropriating upwards of a column, daily, for nearly two weeks, to my use—notwithstanding, with commendable zeal, my opponents had meanwhile secured the public co-operation of a gallant corps of citizen soldiery—"*The Putnam Phalanx*" of Hartford; and that of a body not less intelligent or gallant—*the General Assembly of the State of Connecticut.*

This series of letters having attracted the attention of "the reading public," some of my personal friends have desired, and, unsuccessfully, attempted to obtain, copies of "*The Post*" which contain it; and, at their request, a few copies, for circulation among those who are particularly interested in the subject, have been printed in this form.

In preparing this edition of the letters for the press, I have made no alterations, except to correct the typographical errors which had crept into *my own letters.* Those of my opponent have been printed *without any alteration whatever,* from the fact that their author *has declined my request for corrected copies of his letters,* and I did not feel authorized to make *any* alterations without his approval.

Desiring that this correspondence may receive that indulgence from the reader which the literary labors of all *business men* require; and that "*Selah*" or myself, as our respective productions may merit, will receive the sympathy of "the masses of the people of Connecticut," with whom "the honor of Connecticut" can alone be confided with safety,

I remain,
Respectfully yours,
HENRY B. DAWSON.

MORRISANIA, New York, September 1, 1859.

"SELAH'S" FIRST LETTER.

[From the "Hartford Daily Post," Jan. 27, 1859.]

MAJOR-GENERAL PUTNAM.

It is with feelings of genuine pleasure that we are made aware that there is yet a little of patriotism left in this State of honorable Revolutionary history, and that the spirit of justice and right has not quite all died out—as evinced by so glowing an address as was delivered, a few evenings since, by the Hon. Henry C. Deming, on the life and services of that worthy old hero—Major General Israel Putnam.

We say that it is pleasant to thus witness a man of Mr. Deming's learning and position, coming out from the ranks of lukewarm lovers of heroism, and doing such gallant battle for so worthy an object—not so much for the matter of bandying words upon the subject, as to refute some of the miserably untrue statements that have been put forward by many of the would-be historians of the day, and hurl back in their teeth some of the myriad falsehoods and unkind sarcasms which have flowed so freely from their perjured pens.

To our utter astonishment and sincere grief it was, that we came upon some remarks upon the services of General Putnam during the Revolution, in a new work, entitled

"Battles of the United States by Sea and Land," by HENRY B. DAWSON, that bear such unmistakable evidence of prejudice, rancor and malice, that are penned in such a cutting, sarcastic manner, and that have their paragraphs so thickly interspersed with italics, for the purpose of giving their envenomed dart a doubly poisoned point, that we cannot forbear giving a few extracts, for the purpose of allowing the public to see to what extent one man may disgrace himself in attempting to cast a stigma upon a character so shining and lustrous as was that of General PUTNAM.

The following extracts are *verbatim* from the work itself, bearing the italics as there found.

In speaking of the battle of Brooklyn Heights, Mr. DAWSON, after charging upon General PUTNAM repeated and unpardonable blunders, and alleging that he disregarded all the orders given him from both General WASHINGTON and General SULLIVAN, in reference to the security of the various passes and approaches to the Heights, as also the posting of guards and patrols, and the sending out of scouting parties to reconnoitre the enemy's position—winds up his tirade in the following words:

"And, finally, that to his *ignorant, self-conceited inefficiency* the enemy is indebted for one of the greatest victories of the war, and his country for one of the most disastrous defeats, both military and moral, which it ever experienced."

Is the above true? We sincerely believe it has no foundation in truth, and base our belief on sound and undeniable historical *facts*, too numerous to mention in our brief space.

Passing over many such paragraphs as the one we have

copied above, occurring in various places, in reference to General PUTNAM in the several actions in which he was engaged, we proceed to make some extracts from a brief memoir of the General, in the same work. At the outset—

"ISRAEL PUTNAM was born at Salem, Massachusetts, on the seventh day of January, 1718. . . . . At the age of twenty-one, he removed to Pomfret, Connecticut, where he engaged in the cultivation of a considerable tract of ground, which he had purchased."

Now, is it possible that General PUTNAM was twenty-one years of age when he removed to Pomfret, and yet none know of the occurrence? The oldest inhabitants of Pomfret, and all of the town records, go to prove that he was *born* in that town. Again:

"It was at this place [Pomfret] that the tremendous 'she-wolf,' of which the world has heard so much, killed, it is said, *in one night*, seventy-five sheep and goats of his flock, besides wounding many of his lambs and kids; and there, also, is the wonderful cave where this terrible beast found refuge, and in which Mr. PUTNAM so gallantly confronted and killed her."

We give the above extract, to show the vein of sarcasm and prejudice that pervades the whole article. As still another example of this humor, we have the following, in speaking of him after he had joined the army in the old French War:

"It was in this campaign, while out on a scout near Ticonderoga, that the miraculous escape, so much spoken of, and so well known, occurred. The *folded* blanket which he carried on his back, *when opened*, showed no less than fourteen bullet holes through it."

It is certainly wonderful what a grim satisfaction Mr.

Dawson appears to take in pulling down all of our fair castles in the air, and dispelling those bright visions of a brave and gallant warrior in the form of "Old Put." And now read his words in reference to the battle of Bunker's Hill:

"At the battle of Bunker's Hill, he is said, by his eulogists, to have performed prodigies of valor. Those who were present, admit that he went on the ground with Colonel Prescott and his party, on the evening before the battle, but they agree that he did not remain there. They say he returned on the following morning; but they agree that he ordered the intrenching tools to be removed from the redoubt, in opposition to the remonstrances of Colonel Prescott, and for that purpose withdrew a large number of Colonel Prescott's troops from the redoubt, at a time when the approach of the enemy showed that they were actually needed in the works. When the re-enforcements under Colonel Stark came on the hill, they saw General Putnam and a large body of men quietly standing on the *safe* side of Bunker's Hill, beyond the range of the enemy's artillery; and, when the same body retreated, after the struggle at the works was ended, the General and his men were at the same place, and quietly joined in the retreat."

Here, then, we have the matter in a nut-shell. With any person at all conversant with the character and disposition of General Putnam, the above extract will unhesitatingly be pronounced a falsehood! But, oh! Sons of Connecticut! does it not make the blood in your veins tingle and grow hot to thus have this Mr. Dawson publish to the world that a body of Connecticut men, led by a man whom you have all learned to look up to as a hero— that they were inactive, and " quietly standing on the *safe* side of Bunker's Hill," on that ever-memorable day! It has always been a favorite belief in our mind that *all* the American troops on Bunker's Hill were in warm action, and that there were *no* drones or idlers in the ranks on that day. Must this theory be entirely evaporated by Mr. Dawson? We shall need the proofs first: and those he cannot bring!

Once more, and the last. Not the last for want of material—for this work teems with such unjust remarks—but the last, for want of room, in which to enlarge more freely:

"For his '*gallantry*' at Bunker's Hill, Colonel Prescott—the acknowledged hero of that engagement—some years afterward, at an official dinner with Governor Bowdoin, of Massachusetts, openly declared General Putnam *deserved to be shot!* But those who were *not* there, and whose information is generally acquired from *less* reliable sources, generally suppose the venerable Colonel was mistaken in his conclusions [cool], notwithstanding Colonel Gerrish, in whose company the General was, and whose orders the Colonel was bound to obey, for *this very offense*, was afterwards *arrested for cowardice, tried by a court-martial, cashiered,* and *universally execrated.*"

This is all most pitiable! Were there even a shadow of a doubt that General Putnam did not perform those brave and gallant deeds—that he did not, as the battle alarum came on the winds from the field of Lexington, leave the plow in the furrow, and hasten to the scene of strife, to mingle in the fray—that his heart did not warm and thrill with those generous impulses, and his spirit burn with an intense and unconquerable desire to serve his country, and do battle in an oppressed country's cause;

in short, that he performed none of those brave and gallant actions, and was in no respect the hero that we have all loved to picture him—revolving incidents in his history, in our minds, with an undying admiration—looking at the relics that have been left to us, with a reverential awe, for their associations with him—speaking his name to our children, and teaching them to look up to him for a noble example of native bravery and courage, warm and patriotic attachment to a bleeding country's cause, indefatigable exertions in his command, and a spirit ever undaunted during the heaviest trials and under the most oppressive burdens of care and toil—we say, if there were a shadow of doubt that such was the case, and such the man, we would give that doubt its due weight and force.

But there cannot be found anywhere, save in the garbled works of some prejudiced historians, or in the words and letters of those contemporary officers with PUTNAM, who felt a rancorous and venomous hate for him, because of his glowing actions—actions so unlike their own, in their undoubted justice, and gallantry, and zeal—there cannot be found, we say, the first line, or paragraph, or the first historical *fact*, to prove that General PUTNAM was that "ignorant, self-conceited" and "cowardly" man which Mr. DAWSON labors so hard to represent him.

Three-quarters of a century has rolled away, with all its various mutations and changes, its unrolling of records, and its decyphering of them, and its never-ceasing search into Revolutionary chronicles; yet nothing has been brought to light to detract one jot or tittle from General PÚTNAM's well-earned glory—nor pluck one leaf from the laurel-wreath which encircles his brow, in our minds—or even to raise a just doubt of the validity of his claim to those words of praise, and those feelings of respect and admiration which all true Americans so well love to accord him.

On the other hand, many and many are the incidents—little as distinct and separate, but a Colossus as a whole—that have been dragged forth from the oblivion of some old manuscript or library, or been related by the feeble and faltering tongue of age, uttering reminiscences of childhood's days, when General PUTNAM was a companion and playmate—to speak in thunder-tones to prove the legitimacy of the claim for honor and glory for him " who dared to lead where any dared to follow!"—whose cool intrepidity and dauntless bravery wrought so much toward giving that terrible check to British arms at Bunker's Hill—whose presence and word of command inspired the troops, at Brooklyn Heights, to deeds of utmost daring—whose ready tact, consummate skill, and indomitable energy, lent a Herculean arm to the American cause throughout the war—and won for himself a lofty niche in the Temple of Fame, where every honest heart loves to behold him—and whose name is engraven on the hearts of all Americans, and inscribed on the immortal roll of patriots, in the great Temple of American Liberty!

SELAH.

HENRY B. DAWSON'S FIRST LETTER.

[From the "Hartford Daily Post," Feb. 14, 1859.]

WHITE PLAINS, N. Y., Feb. 5, 1859.

To the Editor of the Hartford Post:

THROUGH the kindness of a friend in New York, I have been favored with a copy of your daily of the 27th ult., in which an anonymous writer, "*Selah*," uses my name, motives, and labors with considerable spirit and freedom.

Having had no doubt that your correspondent feels easier since your publication of his article, I would not have disturbed his quiet or encroached on your space or the time of your readers, had not his remarks found a place in the paper which "has the largest circulation of any daily paper in Connecticut," while they lack the most essential element in such an article—the unalloyed Truth.

The remarks in which he has been pleased to attack me personally; the *general* remarks of "prejudice, rancor and malice," "envenomed darts," with "doubly-poisoned points," "tirade," "no foundation in truth," "falsehood," &c., with which he bespatters my motives and my pages; and the empty declamation, without a single authority, with which he fills nearly two columns of the *Post*, have passed away with the winds which pass down the valley of the Connecticut, and I shall not disturb their flight toward the ocean of oblivion. I may be pardoned, however, if I ask space to notice his *specific* charges, through the same medium in which they were made.

My conclusions on General PUTNAM's character have been formed on "sound and undeniable *facts*," each of which is given, *at length*, in the pages referred to by "*Selah*," with ample authorities, at the foot of each page, to sustain it, all of which, *and many others*, can be found in the Library of the Connecticut Historical Society, and in every respectable private library, in your city. When the worthlessness of these authorities shall have been established, the deductions which have been drawn therefrom will, of course, fall to the ground, and "*Selah*" be recognized as *the* great historical touchstone; until that time, your correspondent will, probably, remain what, so far as this subject goes, he now is—an anonymous scribbler.

My remarks, respecting the place of General PUTNAM's birth, appear to have disturbed "*Selah's*" repose; and Pomfret, Conn., instead of Salem, Mass., is, indirectly, claimed as his birth-place. I have not had access to "the oldest inhabitants" of Pomfret, and "all the town records," which "go to prove that he [General PUTNAM] was *born* in that town." That privilege has been reserved, *solely*, for "*Selah*," I presume; although he modestly conceals the *special* advantage which he has gained, under a *general* assertion. It has been my humble lot, not knowing of "*Selah*," or his aged friends, or more aged town records, to follow the Rev. Dr. ALLEN (*Biographical Dictionary*, 3d ed., p. 685), Dr. THATCHER (*Military Journal*, Appendix, p. 387), Colonel DAVID HUMPHREY's (*Life of Putnam*, p. 8), and the inscription on General PUTNAM's tomb at Brooklyn, Conn., all of which say he was born at Salem, Mass., with which I have been, and am still, perfectly contented.

"*Selah*" cites my remarks on the she-wolf and folded blanket, only "to show the vein of sarcasm and prejudice that pervades the whole article," without even attempting to deny their truth. I need only say that his zeal, to this extent at least, has been compelled to give way, unwillingly, to his discretion.

While commenting on my remarks concerning General PUTNAM's questionable gallantry on Bunker's Hill, "*Selah*" becomes *a falsifier;* and this, Mr. Editor, has mainly influenced me in asking the space in your columns which this note will occupy. *I have never said, or thought,* that "a body of Connecticut men, led by a man whom you have all learned to look up to as a hero, were inactive," and "quietly standing on the safe side of Bunker's Hill," as "*Selah*" falsely insinuates, and his pious ejaculations on the subject, like other parts of his story, pass harmlessly away. I have said that General PUTNAM was on the shady side of the hill, "with a large body of men," whom — as I say four or five lines above — he had withdrawn from Colonel PRESCOTT's force within the redoubt, in which, after they ceased their labor, there had been *no* Connecticut men, and from which, consequently, there could not have been any withdrawn. The Connecticut men were *behind the rail fence* — not in the redoubt; and under the noble THOMAS KNOWLTON, of Ashford, Conn., they did their duty *there*. I have now before me, in the handwriting of that same glorious THOMAS KNOWLTON — compared with whose deeds and patriotism those of ISRAEL PUTNAM are but worthless trash — *the roll of that Ashford Company*, which, under his command, on the banks of the Mystic, June 17th, 1775, secured for PUTNAM and Connecticut what both have since enjoyed, but neither acknowledged.

When I look on this interesting relic; read the remarks which appear on the margin, opposite the names of those who fell on that memorable day; and examine the accounts, and receipts for pay, and, sometimes, for "sarse-money" of the survivors; and then glance over "*Selah's*" appeal to the "Sons of Connecticut," as the conservators of the honor of Connecticut, I cannot avoid the reflection that this same purely patriotic KNOWLTON, and many of the signers of these receipts, fell in a successful attempt to restore the honor of Connecticut, which had been trailed in the dust at Kipp's Bay; that they all now rest without a stone, or even a stake, to mark their burial places; and that "*Selah*" and his "Sons of Connecticut" (in their "reverential awe" of the "relics" of General PUTNAM) appear to have forgotten, if they ever knew, that THOMAS KNOWLTON, JOHN KEYES and DANIEL ALLEN, and their men, ever lived or died for the honor of Connecticut.

"*Selah's*" wonted discretion shows itself in the empty declamation with which he condemns my remarks on General PUTNAM's "gallantry" on Bunker's Hill, and it needs no particular notice from me. If it will gratify him, however, I may be allowed to say, that *it is not true* that General PUTNAM performed " those brave and gallant deeds" referred to by " *Selah*," or any of them; that *he did not*, " as the battle alarm came on the winds from the field of Lexington, leave the plow in the furrow, and hasten to the scene of strife, to mingle in the fray;" that his heart *did not* " warm and thrill with those generous impulses, and his spirit burn with an intense and unconquerable desire to serve his country;" that *no* " works of *prejudiced* historians" or of *envious* contemporary officers, either " garbled" or complete, are required to establish " the ignorant, self-conceited inefficiency of General Putnam," or the truth of Colonel Prescott's charge against his gallantry at Bunker's Hill—nor will they be required for such a purpose, while the names and words of John Stark, David Wooster, John Sullivan, George Clinton, and George Washington are remembered; or the slopes at Gowanus or the rocky heights on the Highlands remain undisturbed : and, finally, that until the connection between General Putnam and Majors Small and Moncrieffe of the Royal army, and the charges of a questionable intimacy with the enemy, which Robert R. Livingston preferred against the General (*Letter to General Washington*, January 14, 1778), remain unexplained, as they now are, "*Selah*" might reasonably select some other, if not more fitting object, for his "hero-worship," and as the representative of Revolutionary Connecticut.

I am a stranger to nearly all your neighbors—the only resident of Hartford with whom I am personally acquainted is, I believe, now in Rome—and I would be sorry to consider "*Selah*" a fair representative of that ancient and respectable town. An examination of my sentiments, and of the authorities which I refer to in support of them, as well as the production *of evidence* to disprove my statements, is invited and expected. I was *not* prepared, however, to find in the columns of a widely-circulating journal, published in a distant city, a personal assault such as this; and I am consoled with the reflection that its author, conscious of his own dishonor, masks his identity under the cloak of the "Psalmist of Israel." With his acknowledged "reverential awe," when in the presence of the "relics" of such departed worthies as General Putnam; with his steady rejection of the *written* authority, when it interferes with the traditions of the fathers; with the customary multiplication of birth-places for his saint, as is usual with such people; and with his practical justification of the means in the accomplishment of the end, the locality of "*Selah*" is easily determined; and I leave him with his fraternity, and with your readers, to be rewarded as they may, severally, see fit.

Respectfully, Yours,
HENRY B. DAWSON.

"SELAH'S" SECOND LETTER.

[From the "Hartford Daily Post," February 23, 1859.]

To the Editor of the Hartford Daily Post:

In your issue of the 5th inst., I find a letter from Mr. DAWSON, in which he indulges to an excessive degree in gasconade and self-esteem, in an unavailing attempt to fortify an untenable position which he saw fit to take in his work, the "Battles of the United States by Sea and Land." In that work he took it upon himself to belabor and stigmatize, in an unjust and unwarrantable manner, the life and services of General ISRAEL PUTNAM. In an issue of your paper for the 27th ult., I made reference to this spirit of prejudice and ill-will toward General PUTNAM, as evinced by Mr. DAWSON in the compilation of his work, and gave several quotations from the same, upon which I took the liberty to make some strictures, commenting upon them, pronouncing them false in their sentiment and design, and stating that no proof could be produced to verify his statements—*as I do now, most emphatically.*

Mr. DAWSON in his letter charges me with a personal attack upon him. I had hoped that he was a man of too good sense to be led away with so ridiculous an idea. Every man who issues from the press a work treating upon history, is *responsible* for what he has said therein. And if his work will not bear the eye and pen of criticism, it is worth but little. Now, if to comment upon the sentiments and tenor of that work is to "personally assault" the author of it, then I have assaulted Mr. DAWSON; and, if such be the effect of criticism, it is a thing entirely new to me. But enough of this.

Mr. DAWSON, after referring to several works, to be used as "authorities" to prove my statements false, and render the name of PUTNAM infamous, (some of which I shall refer to *to prove the* REVERSE,) he makes use of the following scandalous language:

"If it will gratify him, however, I may be allowed to say that *it is not true* that Gen. PUTNAM performed 'those brave and gallant deeds' referred to by 'Selah,' or any of them; that *he did not* 'as the battle alarm came on the winds from the battle of Lexington, leave the plough in the furrow, and hasten to the scene of strife, to mingle in the fray;' that his heart *did not* 'warm and thrill with those generous impulses, and his spirit burn with an intense and unconquerable desire to serve his country;' that *no* 'works of *prejudiced* historians, or of *envious* cotemporary officers,' either 'garbled' or complete, are required to establish 'the ignorant, self-conceited inefficiency of Gen. PUTNAM,' or the truth of Col. PRESCOTT'S charge against his gallantry at Bunker's Hill."

Now, this is so exceedingly absurd, so rankling with prejudice, and so overloaded with untruth, that it does really seem sheer nonsense to make any reply to it. Nor is this my opinion barely; others, far better versed in the history of our country than I ever expect to be, look upon it in the same light, and express themselves in the same manner. But, lest some may read the sentiments of Mr. DAWSON, and, being ignorant of the *facts* in the premises, accept them as the law, I feel myself constrained to give a few quotations from *undoubted* authorities, and so allow the public to see what a mass of evidence and what a host of vouchers that gentleman has set his face against, for the purpose of carrying on his disgraceful war against the unspotted reputation of a Hero of the Revolution, long since gathered to the dust of his fathers.

The works from which I quote are to be obtained at any book-store and in any library, and all may refer to them, that they may satisfy themselves of the accuracy of my quoting, and the authority I have for pronouncing Mr. DAWSON's statements utterly false and untenable.

In reference to PUTNAM's adventures in the French War, I find the following in Dr. ALLEN's "American Biographical Dictionary:"

"During the French War, he was appointed to command a company of the first troops which were raised in Connecticut, in 1755. He rendered much service to the army in the neighborhood of Crown Point. In 1756, while near Ticonderoga, he was repeatedly in the most imminent danger. He escaped, in an adventure of one night, *with twelve bullet-holes in his blanket.*"

Whereabouts in this paragraph, Mr. DAWSON, does he say that the plurality of bullet-holes was occasioned by the folded state of his blanket? Besides, the number of bullet-holes was *twelve,* and not *fourteen,* as stated in your work. Mr. DAWSON, you do not *copy* your work correctly!

The author of "Washington and the Generals of the Revolution," in speaking of the above adventure, in which PUTNAM was accompanied by a comrade in arms, by the name of DURKEE, who was wounded, says:

"Amid a shower of bullets, they succeeded in reaching a spot of safety; but, when PUTNAM came to offer his canteen of brandy to his wounded companion, he discovered that one of the enemy's balls had pierced and emptied it, and his blanket presented no less than twelve bullet-holes, received during their escape."

In reference to the Battle of Lexington, Dr. ALLEN has the following:

"He was ploughing in his field, in 1775, when he heard the news of the Battle of Lexington. He immediately unyoked his team, left his plough on the spot, and, without changing his clothes, set off for Cambridge. He soon went back to Connecticut, levied a regiment, and repaired again to the camp. In a little time he was promoted to the rank of Major-General. In the Battle of Bunker's Hill he exhibited his usual intrepidity. He *directed* the men to reserve their fire till the enemy was very near—reminded them of their skill—and told them to take good aim. They did so, and the execution was terrible. After the retreat, he made a stand at Winter Hill, and drove back the enemy under cover of their ship."

In reference to Gen. PUTNAM's coolness and bravery, as well as promptitude and unwavering decisiveness in cases of emergency, we have the following well-known incident, as related in Dr. ALLEN's work:

"One PALMER, a lieutenant in the Tory new levies, was detected in the camp. Governor TRYON reclaimed him as a British officer, threatening vengeance if he was not restored. Gen. PUTNAM wrote the following pithy reply: 'Sir—NATHAN PALMER, a lieutenant in your King's service, was taken in my camp as a spy; he was tried as a spy; he was condemned as a spy; and he shall be hanged as a spy. P. S.—Afternoon. He is hanged!'"

So much for Dr. ALLEN, one of the "authorities" noticed by Mr. DAWSON as helping to brand Gen. PUTNAM as a coward and poltroon. And now for Gen. HUMPHREY, in his "Life of PUTNAM," (another one of DAWSON's "authorities,") who, referring to PUTNAM's exploit in the wolf-den, makes use of the following language:

"Then it was that the master, [PUTNAM, in reference to his negro man,] angry at the disappointment, and declaring that he *was ashamed to have a coward in his family*, resolved himself to destroy the ferocious beast, lest she should escape through some unknown fissure of the rock," &c.

In BOTTA's "War of the Independence," Vol. I, page 204, I find the following in regard to the Battle of Bunker's Hill, during which action Mr. DAWSON asserts that PUTNAM had no command, and took no part:

"A few moments before the action commenced, Dr. WARREN, who had been appointed a general, a personage of great authority and a zealous patriot, arrived with some reinforcements. Gen. POMEROY made his appearance at the same time. The first joined the troops of his own province of Massachusetts; the second took command of those from Connecticut. Gen. PUTNAM *directed in chief!* and held himself ready to repair to any point where his presence should be most wanted."

In another place, BOTTA affirms that the Connecticut troops, during that battle, were in the trenches, in the very thickest of the fray. Mr. DAWSON declares that they were skulking behind rail-fences. Trying to dodge the bullets, eh? Poor, "cowardly," "dastardly," "treacherous" Connecticut troops! Does your fate and your history hang at the point of Mr. DAWSON's perjured pen? God forbid!

The following is from the pen of Dr. DWIGHT, the eloquent eulogist of Gen. PUTNAM:

"It is not so extensively known as it ought to be that Gen. PUTNAM *commanded* the American forces at the battle of Bunker's Hill; and that to his *courage* and *conduct* the United States are particularly indebted for the advantages of that day; one of the most brilliant in the annals of this country."

In the work "Washington and the Generals of the Revolution," I find the following emphatic words, to strengthen my assertion as to PUTNAM's commandership at that battle:

"After the full accounts given of this event, it is needless to enter into details. Gen. PUTNAM was there, and Gen. WARREN volunteered his services, and even offered to receive the orders of PUTNAM, who recommended him to the redoubt where Col. PRESCOTT was stationed. In this most important conflict, in which the brave and lamented WARREN fell, PUTNAM *was the only general officer in command*, and the battle seems to have been conducted under his guidance; nor is it too much to say that most of the influence exercised by its results may be ascribed to his courage, zeal, and indefatigable efforts."

The following is a piece of unquestioned proof, as the date and circumstances of it will vouch for. It is from the cotemporary press of the Revolution, and is found in Mr. FRANK MOORE's forthcoming "Diary of the Revolution:"

"JUNE 17, 1775.—Last evening, Colonel PUTNAM took possession of Bunker's Hill, with about two thousand men, and began an entrenchment, which they had made some progress in, when, at eight o'clock this morning, a party of regulars landed at Charlestown, and fired that town in different places. Under cover of the smoke, a body of about five thousand men marched up to the American entrenchments and made a furious and sudden attack. They were driven back three times, and when they were making the third attack, one of the Americans imprudently spoke aloud that 'their powder was all gone;' which being heard by some of the regular officers, they encouraged their men to walk up to their trenches, with fixed bayonets, and entered them, on which the Americans were ordered to retreat, which they did with all speed, till they got out of musket shot. They then formed, but were not pursued. [Extract of a letter from a gentleman in Providence to a gentleman in Philadelphia.]—*Pennsylvania Journal*, June 28, 1775.

Mr. DAWSON makes a jest and a jeer of Gen. PUTNAM's bold descent of the hill at Horseneck, now called "PUTNAM's Hill." In the "Connecticut Historical Collections" I find the following very emphatic account of that daring feat:

"On the approach of Gov. TRYON to this place, with a force of about fifteen hundred men, [Gen. PUTNAM planted two iron field-pieces by the meeting-house, without horses or drag ropes. Having fired his cannon several times, PUTNAM, perceiving the British dragoons (supported by the infantry,) about to charge, ordered his men, about one hundred and fifty in number, to provide for their safety, and secured his own by *plunging down the precipice at full trot!* The dragoons, who were but a sword's length from him, stopped short; *for the declivity was so abrupt that they dared not follow!*"

Soon after the Battle of Bunker's Hill, Gen. PUTNAM was raised in rank above Generals WOOSTER and SPENCER, who were of a superior grade. This supersedeas touched the feelings of those gentlemen, more especially SPENCER, who resigned his commission. Gov. TRUMBULL, of this State, acting under instructions from the General Assembly, wrote to Congress, at Philadelphia, in regard to SPENCER's resignation; and from that letter I quote the following sentence, which speaks volumes in favor of PUTNAM's efficiency:

"At the same time, they have the highest sense of Gen. PUTNAM's *singular merit and services*, and request, if it be practicable, that some method may be devised to obviate the difficulties that are apprehended."

I might go on making quotations without end, for the material and authorities are almost endless; but it must be evident to Mr. DAWSON, as well as to all others, that such may not be the case—although my will is good enough to give every scrap and iota of proof that can bear upon the subject—that it is absolutely necessary that all articles that find their way into the columns of a daily paper should be brief as possible. Mr. DAWSON called for the proofs of my assertions as to the falsity of his statements. Have I not given them? True, many more to the point might be given; but do not those that are to be found in this article suffice to prove my assertions? I will now merely say that Gen. PUTNAM's numerous adventures and daring exploits are too well known and relied upon by the mass of people in this State, to have even a shadow of doubt thrown upon the truth of the records by *any historical writer whatever!* and that, in regard to the part taken by him in the Battle of Bunker's Hill, we must say, with a contemporary press, that, "outside of Boston, we presume there are few persons, of common intelligence, who entertain any doubt about it." In regard to Dawson's charge of "self-conceited inefficiency," the very charge is so at variance with all the authorities quoted, and so evidently tinctured with the plague of prejudice, that it cannot be entertained by any reasonable mind for an instant. In regard to the character of the hero, the words of Dr. Dwight speak a volume of eloquence and truth. He says:

"Every employment in which he engaged he filled with reputation. In the private circle of life—as a husband, father, friend and companion—he was alike respected and beloved. In his manners, though somewhat more direct and blunt than most persons who had received an early polished education, he was gentlemanly, and very agreeable. In his disposition, he was sincere, tender-hearted, generous and noble. It is not known that the passion of fear ever found a place in his breast. His word was regarded as an ample security for anything for which it was pledged; and his uprightness commanded absolute confidence. His intellect was vigorous, and his wit pungent, yet pleasant and sportive. * * * During the gayest and most thoughtless period of his life, he still regarded religion with profound reverence, and read the Scriptures with the deepest veneration. In the decline of his life, he publicly confessed the religion of the Gospel, and, in the opinion of the respectable clergyman of Brooklyn, Rev. Dr. Whiting, from whose mouth I received the information, he died hopefully a Christian."

On his tomb-stone I find the following beautiful inscription, a fitting tribute to the memory of a departed hero:

"Passenger, if thou art a soldier, go not away till thou hast dropped a tear over the dust of a Hero, who, ever tenderly attentive to the lives and happiness of his men, dared to lead where any dared to follow. If thou art a Patriot, remember with gratitude how much thou and thy country owe to the disinterested and gallant exertions of the Patriot who sleeps beneath this marble. If thou art an honest, generous, and worthy man, render a sincere and cheerful tribute of respect to a man whose generosity was singular, whose honesty was proverbial, and who, with a slender education, with small advantages, and without powerful friends, raised himself to esteem, and to offices of eminent distinction, by personal worth, and by the diligent services of a useful life!"

In concluding this article, I must remark that I presume many will make the inquiry—"But what motive has Mr. DAWSON in thus attempting to villify the fame and character of Gen. PUTNAM?" Of this I have no absolute knowledge; I can only conjecture the general reason (which has actuated one or two other New York historians, as well as FROTHINGHAM, and others, of Massachusetts,) of envy! "Envy of what?" you will ask. Envy of Gen. PUTNAM's fair fame as a *Connecticut man;* jealousy of the noble part taken by a Connecticut man, and by Connecticut troops, on the soil of Massachusetts, on the one hand, and a bitter feeling engendered in the hearts of New Yorkers, at the fact that Connecticut troops, under the gallant Gen. LEE, preserved the city of New York from being given up to the enemy by its Tory inhabitants, as also the preservation of the Highlands, and the whole Hudson valley, by the troops from Connecticut, posted there throughout the war.   SELAH.

HENRY B. DAWSON'S SECOND LETTER.

[FROM THE "HARTFORD DAILY POST," MARCH 11 AND 12, 1859.]

WHITE PLAINS, N. Y., March 4, 1859.

To the Editor of the Hartford Post:

I HAVE been favored with a copy of the second article which "*Selah*" has addressed to you respecting my statements concerning Gen. ISRAEL PUTNAM, and I respectfully ask a renewal of that indulgence with which you have heretofore favored me, in being allowed a hearing in reply.

I am not surprised that "*Selah*" affects ignorance of the difference between a "*critic*" and a "*personal assailant,*" in his commendable desire to be recognized as the one, rather than to bear the brand of the other. If the charges of "prejudice," "rancor," "malice," "falsehood," "perjury," &c., with which I have been assailed, in "*Selah's*" first article, are truly specimens of legitimate "*criticism,*" and do not constitute a "*personal assault,*" I confess I did not before know what constituted either the one or the other. An examination of the *statements* contained in a work, and a like examination of the *motives* which influenced the writer in making them, constitute two entirely distinct subjects which should not be confounded, even by "*Selah.*" In fact, these two are so entirely independent, that a positive untruth can be written and published with the most honorable and honest purposes, while the matter itself is still *untrue*, and can never be made to possess any other character. I leave the subject, however, for other and more interesting portions of "*Selah's*" letter.

In his first article, he claimed indirectly that Gen. PUTNAM was born in Pomfret, Connecticut, and, in my reply, I cited Dr. ALLEN, Dr. THATCHER, Col. HUMPHREYS, and the General's tomb, to establish the truth of my statement that he was born in Salem, Massachusetts, *and for no other purpose whatever*, as an examination of my remarks will fully prove. With the greatest coolness, worthy of his great examplar, "*Selah*" says I employed them "to render the name of PUTNAM infamous," and "as helping to brand Gen. PUTNAM as a coward and poltroon." If an establishment of the fact that Gen. PUTNAM was born at Salem, Massachusetts, likewise established, simultaneously, that he was "a coward and poltroon," or "rendered the name of PUTNAM infamous," as "*Selah*" intimates, it would appear that the natives of Salem—even those who emigrated to Connecticut and received her homage—were predestinated to infamy and dishonor, an idea from which I entirely dissent. It may be proper to add, in this connection, that as Gen. PUTNAM was really *born in Salem*, ("*Selah's*" "oldest inhabitants" and "town records" to the contrary notwithstanding,) and therefore—"*Selah*" being my authority—was "a coward and poltroon," and an "infamous" character, it would appear, from his own confession, that my ingenuous opponent has become the voluntary friend and the recognized "champion" of disreputable characters, a class of people which is always the most noisy respecting its honor, without ever *showing* that it possesses any.

I am happy in having been the means of diverting "*Selah's*" attention from less worthy objects to the study of the history of his country and the "epitaphs of her sons;" and it affords me pleasure to find that, from the bluster of empty words, he has so far descended from his airy flights that he has been enabled to cite *some* "authorities" to sustain his positions. I thank him for this display of the riches of his library, and the extent of his reading, taking the liberty to suggest, however, that a few "undoubted authorities," besides those to which he has referred, may possibly be found "in any library and in any book store," and "*Selah*" may be edified and possibly enlightened by a continuation of his investigations.

To my denial that "Gen. PUTNAM performed those brave and gallant deeds," &c., "*Selah*" opposes the General's services in the French War, and cites Dr. ALLEN and Dr. GRISWOLD; the wolf story, sustained by Col. HUMPHREYS; his services on Bunker Hill, with BOTTA, DWIGHT, GRISWOLD, and "a gentleman in Providence" as authorities; and his Horse-neck affair, sustained by BARBER's Historical Collections. To my remarks respecting the General's leaving his plough in the furrow and hastening to Lexington, he interposes Dr. ALLEN's Dictionary; to my impeachment of the General's patriotism, he interposes Dr. DWIGHT and the General's epitaph; and these, with some few minor interludes, constitute the whole of "*Selah's*" response. In asking space to notice these several points, I disclaim any fear that "*Selah*" will "be taken as the law," regretting that I cannot reciprocate his good opinion of my last letter in that respect. My only object is to *establish the truth;* and if the testimony which I propose to submit to "the mass of the people of Connecticut"—in this case the umpires between "*Selah*" and myself—is less reliable or less weighty than that adduced by my opponent, none will submit with a better grace, or retire from the contest with greater satisfaction than I. It is a work of but little pleasure, and certainly of no profit, to strip from the brows of those who have worn them, the laurels which they have stolen from other and better men; yet the duty which falls upon all who pretend to write the history of their country, leaves no other course for them to pursue; and I trust that I will not be found wanting either in my respect for "established reputations," or in the discharge of my duty in connection with them. But to a brief notice of "*Selah's*" article.

I. Respecting the General's services in the French War, my authorities will be brief, but, I trust, conclusive. An examination of the reports of the scouting parties, in 1755, will show that, during that year, Captain ISRAEL PUTNAM was sent out on four several scouts—twice as a subordinate with Major ROGERS, and twice with independent commands. Three of these, as will be seen by the *Reports*, dated Oct. 9, Oct. 22, and Nov. 15, were not productive of any honor, because Capt. PUTNAM kept out of all danger; the other, which was commanded by Major ROGERS, has attracted more attention. On the second of November, while Capt. PUTNAM was concealed on the margin of the lake, watching two canoes, which had been sent out on his front as decoys, especially for that purpose, the main body of the Indians—like Sir WM. HOWE and Sir HENRY CLINTON, some years afterwards—stole upon his rear, and then, as in later times, he found safety ——— *in running*. It was in this affair the Indians "Shot Thro' his Blanket in Divers Places," and, by reference to the document (*Report of Capt.*

Rogers & Co., "*Camp at Lake George, Nov.* 3, 1755,") "*Selah*" may possibly determine whether there were twelve or fourteen holes in it; and, by extending his investigations, he may also possibly determine whether the Captain's face or his back was toward the enemy, when his blanket was thus perforated.

I may also be permitted to invite "*Selah's*" attention to HUMPHREYS' *Life of Putnam*, Ed. Phila., 1798, pp. 20, 21, respecting my correctness in *copying*. The author, after describing, in his peculiar manner, the exploit of Nov. 2, 1755, to which I have referred, and the apocryphal adventure with Lieut. DURKEE, says: "There they betook themselves to a large log, by the side of which they lodged the remainder of the night. Before they laid down, PUTNAM said he had a little rum in his canteen, which would never be more acceptable or necessary; but on examining the canteen, which hung under his arm, he found the enemy had pierced it with their balls, and there was not a drop of liquor left. The next day he found *fourteen* bullet holes in his blanket." Any school-boy can tell "*Selah*" that a soldier's blanket is always *folded* and carried on his *back*, during the day and during action; and, while that fact is known, no other evidence is required to prove that the blanket was shot through while it was *folded*, and while its owner had *his back to the foe.*

Without occupying your space with unnecessary details, allow me to pass from 1755 to 1759—from *Capt.* PUTNAM's exploits as a new recruit, in his first campaign, which we have just noticed, to *Lieut. Col.* PUTNAM, a veteran of five years' active duty, and, if "*Selah*" is correct, of brilliant achievements. In 1759, we find him in camp among his old associates, and his gallant services, if he had performed any, could not have failed to have secured for him the confidence of his commander. Under any circumstances, he would have been assigned to duties which corresponded, in character and importance, with his intellectual and professional abilities; and the records will show how the veteran was employed. The Order Books of the army (*After Orders, Fort Edward, 19th June,* 1759,) show that he was ordered to take the command of "eight hundred working Men for mending the Roads to the 4 Mile Post." At the same time, however, Lieut. REBIER was ordered to "attend to direct the Work," the Commander of the Expedition — evidently supposing that PUTNAM had not sufficient intelligence to "direct the work" of an ordinary country roadmaster, in filling the ruts and gullies—leaving to the Lieut. Colonel no other duty than that of sitting on a log, whittling a stick, and hurrying onward those of his party who were disposed to be idle. On the 15th of July, in the same year, two hundred working men were assigned to "Lieut. Col. PUTNAM to finish his Garden," with permission "to take what Tools he directs." (*General Orders, Lake George, 15th July,* 1759.) And, on the 8th August, "with 334 Provincialls," he was sent out of the camp *to cut wood*, and in this employment he continued during the remainder of the season. If "*Selah*" desires the details of this wood-cutting hero's campaign during the latter part of 1759, he can find them in the Order Books of the army, (*General Orders, Aug.* 8, 12, 13, 20, 27 ; *Sept.* 3, 10, 17, 24 ; *Oct.* 1, 6, 9, 22, and 30, 1759 ;) and if he and "the mass of the people of Connecticut," for whom he assumes to speak, are content to worship such an idol as *this*, it is their own business, not mine ; yet I may be allowed to remark, that the noble School Fund of that State leads those who are disinterested to hope for a different result.

II. Respecting the wolf story, I had supposed that it had been so far exploded that none at this late day would seriously offer it as an evidence of the bravery of Gen. PUTNAM. I shall not insult your readers so far as to repeat the refutations which have already appeared, most of which will be obvious to any intelligent person who reads the story. I cannot deny myself the privilege, however, of copying, for "*Selah's*" especial benefit, a description of "the wonderful cave where this terrible beast found refuge, and in which Mr. PUTNAM so gallantly confronted and killed her." *The Historical Magazine*, Vol. 2, page 20, after describing a visit of the writer with a party of students from Providence, to this locality, and repeating the substance of Col. HUMPHREYS' description of the cave, says: "Now, *in reality*, it is all of three feet square at the mouth, and descends, at a small inclination, for about twenty feet. Here the rocks are entirely closed up, and no opening could be found, though, for at least half an hour, we dug earnestly. The tradition among the people is, that it extends much farther into the hill." As this description is confirmed by others, who have also visited the spot, I leave it for "*Selah*" to determine how long the "rope" must have been which was said to have been tied to PUTNAM's legs when he crept into this remarkable den.

III. Respecting the part which Gen. PUTNAM took on Bunker Hill, "*Selah*" appears to be peculiarly sensitive; but we are not indebted to his "undoubted authorities" alone for our knowledge of that subject. BOTTA, an Italian writer, who never saw America, after having passed through the filter of an American translation; DWIGHT, whose sermons and theology are more reliable than his history; GRISWOLD, whose forte was not historical research; and "a gentleman in Providence," who does not pretend to anything but "hearsay evidence," and whose errors are manifest to every one, are well enough as far as they go, and would have been better had we no other and more reliable evidence to contradict their statements. Can "*Selah*" possibly suppose that all that relates to Bunker Hill and its heroes is concentrated in BOTTA, DWIGHT, GRISWOLD, and "the gentleman in Providence?" Let us see what those who were personally present, and the contemporary writers say on the subject. The Provincial Congress of Massachusetts, under whose authority Bunker Hill was occupied, in its official communication on that subject to the Continental Congress (*In Provincial Congress, Watertown, June* 20, 1775,) and in its reply to the Albany Committee of Safety, when the latter body inquired for the details of the engagement (*Minutes of the Congress, Wednesday, June* 28, 1775); the Massachusetts Committee of Safety, (in its very full "*Account of the late battle at Charlestown,*" dated July 25, 1775); Capt. ELIJAH HIDE, of Lebanon, Connecticut, who was a spectator of the scene, (*Account of an engagement near Charlestown, &c.*); Governor JONATHAN TRUMBULL, of Connecticut, of whose facilities for obtaining correct information concerning passing events "*Selah*" can easily satisfy himself (*Letters to the Baron J. D. Van der Capellan,* "*Lebanon,* 31 *August,* 1779," in which he also assigns the command of the troops to "*the brave Gen. Warren*"); the author of the "*Narrative of the action, which was in Cambridge, Mass., June* 22, 1775;" General FOLSOM, of New Hampshire, in his report to the Committee of Safety of that Province, (*Letter dated* "*Med-*

ford, June 22, 1775"); ISAAC LATHROP, at Watertown, (*Letter to Thaddeus Burr, Fairfield, Conn., dated* "June 22, 1775," and by the latter on the 25th sent to General WOOSTER) ; Governor JOHN BROOKS, of Massachusetts, who was a Captain in Col. BRIDGE's regiment, and a volunteer with Col. PRESCOTT, during the whole of Friday night, and until the close of the action (" *Particulars respecting the action,*" &c.) ; Col. JOHN STARK, who commanded a regiment behind the rail-fence during the battle, (*Letter to the Provincial Congress of New Hampshire,*" *Medford, June 22,* 1775") ; Captain JOHN CHESTER, who commanded a company of Connecticut troops behind the fence during the battle, (*Letter to Rev. Joseph Fish,* " *Cambridge, July 22,* 1775") ; PETER BROWN, a private in Col. PRESCOTT's regiment, on the hill in the battle, (*Letter to his mother,* " *Cambridge, June 25,* 1775") ; SAMUEL GRAY, who from his language appears to have been on the hill in the battle, (*Letter to Mr. Dyer,* " *Roxbury, July* 12, 1775") ; Col. WILLIAM PRESCOTT, the illustrious " hero of Bunker Hill," (*Letter to John Adams,* " *Camp at Cambridge, August* 25, 1775") ; Chief Justice MARSHALL, an officer of the Revolutionary army, (*Life of Washington,* Edit. London, 1804, 2, pp. 289–297) ; General HENRY LEE, of Virginia, also an officer of the same army, (*Memoirs,* Edit. Washington, 1827, pp. 33–34) ; Mrs. MERCY WARREN, the sister of JAMES OTIS, and the wife of President JAMES WARREN, (*Hist. of American Revolution,* 1, pp. 217–222) ; to say nothing of more recent writers, make no allusion whatever to PUTNAM, in connexion with the battle of Bunker Hill ; while some of them assign the command, either in part or altogether, to other persons. These citations prove what I desire them to prove—that " in the times which tried men's souls," and among those who were present on Bunker Hill, or immediately connected with it, PUTNAM was not considered a prominent actor in that engagement, in any capacity, or entitled to "special mention" in the narratives of that event.

From this branch of the subject let us turn to another chapter in the history of Bunker's Hill. On the 17th of March, 1776, JAMES WILKINSON— afterwards a Major-General in the Army of the United States—walked over the field of action, with Colonels JOHN STARK and JAMES REED, of New Hampshire, who, with THOMAS KNOWLTON, of Connecticut, commanded the troops who were behind the rail-fence in the battle; and, *on their authority*, he states (*Memoirs of his own Times*, vol. 1, pp. 32-3; 841-7) that when the reinforcements, under Colonel STARK, came to the ground, before the battle, General PUTNAM was standing on the safe side of Bunker's Hill, with entrenching tools slung across his horse, and Colonel GERRISH by his side; that they remained there *inactive*, and with a large body of men, while the battle continued; and that, when the troops retreated, the General, and those who were with him, quietly fell into the current and retreated with the others, without attempting to cover the retreat, or to assist the fugitives. The account is too long to be copied here; but its substance appears in the following words of General HENRY DEARBORN, who was a Captain in Colonel JOHN STARK's regiment, marched over Charlestown Neck by the side of his Colonel, and fought on the extreme right of the line which occupied the fence: "In the battle of Bunker's Hill, he (General PUTNAM) took post on *the declivity towards Charlestown Neck*, where *I saw* him on horseback, as we passed on to Breed's Hill, with Colonel GERrish by his side. *I heard* the gallant Colonel PRESCOTT (who commanded in the redoubt) observe, after the war, at the table of his Excellency JAMES BOWDOIN, then Governor of this Commonwealth, 'that he sent three messengers during the battle to General PUTNAM, requesting him to come forward and take the command, there being no general present, and the relative rank of Colonel not having been settled; but that he received no answer, and his whole conduct was such, both during the action and the retreat, that he had ought to have been shot.' He remained at or near the top of Bunker's Hill until the retreat, with Col. GERRISH by his side. *I saw them* together when we retreated. He not only continued at that distance himself during the whole of the action, but had a force with him nearly as large as that engaged. No reinforcement of men or ammunition was sent to our assistance; and instead of attempting to cover the retreat of those who had expended their last shot in the face of the enemy, he retreated in company with Colonel GERRISH, and his whole force, without discharging a single musket; but what is still more astonishing, Colonel GERRISH was arrested for cowardice, tried, cashiered, and universally execrated, while not a word was said against the conduct of General PUTNAM, whose extraordinary popularity alone saved him, not only from trial, but even from censure." * * *

"When General PUTNAM's ephemeral and unaccountable popularity subsided or faded away, and the minds of the people were released from the shackles of a delusive trance, the circumstances relating to Bunker's Hill were viewed or talked of in a very different light, and the selection of the unfortunate Colonel GERRISH as a *scape-goat*, considered as a mysterious and inexplicable event." There is also ample corroboration of this in General HEATH's words (*Memoirs*, p. 19). "Just before the action began, General PUTNAM came to the redoubt, and told Colonel PRESCOTT that the entrenching tools should be sent off, or they would be lost. The Colonel replied that if he sent any of the men away with the tools, not one of them would return. To this the General answered, 'they shall every man return.' A large party was then sent off with the tools, and not one of them returned," as General STARK, WILKINSON and DEARBORN have related.

There is still another chapter in the history of Bunker's Hill which "*Selah*" may study with profit; and after having opened that, and noticed a little interlude connected with the battle, I propose to dismiss the subject. In chapter V. of "*The Battles of the United States*," I have given to Colonel PRESCOTT the chief command; while Generals WARREN, POMEROY and PUTNAM, as *volunteers*, without command, are also said to have been on the field *before* the action. The two former remained there during the day—one in the redoubt and the other behind the fence; but PUTNAM retired before the battle began, taking with him the intrenching tools and part of Colonel PRESCOTT's men, to carry them—neither the men or the General appearing afterwards. The retirement from the field and subsequent *inactivity* of General PUTNAM having been already noticed, I need only call "*Selah's*" attention to the following "undoubted authorities," from contemporary evidence, respecting the question of the commander: Governor JOHN BROOKS, Generals WILLIAM HEATH, HENRY LEE, JAMES WILKINSON and HENRY DEARBORN, whose several testimonies have been already referred to; Rev. JOHN MARTIN, "who was in the thickest of it," (*Communicated to Prest.*

Stiles, of Yale College, and entered in his *Diary*, June 30, 1775); Hon. JOHN PITTS, an influential member of the Committee of Safety, (*Letter to Samuel Adams*, "*Watertown, July* 20, 1775"); Dr. JAMES THATCHER, of the Revolutionary army, (*Military Journal*, pp. 26, 29); Hon. WILLIAM TUDOR, Judge Advocate, who tried Colonel GERRISH and other delinquent officers, (*Columbian Centinal, July* 11, 1818); Dr. WILLIAM GORDON, whose personal acquaintance with the New England officers at that time gave him great facilities for obtaining correct information (*Hist. of Am. Revolution*, Ed. London, 1788, 2, p. 39), Chief Justice MARSHALL, (*Life of Washington*, Ed. London, 1804, 2, p. 289); and DANIEL WEBSTER, *North American Review*, July, 1818); to say nothing of the complete work of Mr. FROTHINGHAM, (*Siege of Boston*), and other modern writers — all sustain me in assigning to Colonel PRESCOTT the chief command, and in claiming for him the honor of having been " the hero of Bunker's Hill."

The interlude to which I have referred is that in which "*Selah*" tries "to keep his courage up," by whistling over the rail-fence. His assertion that I had "declared" that " the Connecticut troops were SKULKING behind rail fences," does not affect me in the least; and, if it was not perfectly evident that "*Selah*" is ignorant of the details of the action, I should pass the subject, with the silent contempt which it merits. I am not surprised, however, that "*Selah*" is ignorant of the locality of the rail-fence on the banks of the Mystic, where THOMAS KNOWLTON, and such of the Connecticut troops AS DID THEIR DUTY, were stationed, and where WILLIAM CHENEY, ASHEL LYON, and BENJAMIN RUSS laid down their lives for the defense of their country. That spot is holy ground, rendered sacred by the presence and the blood of patriotic yeomanry, who battled nobly, and, in some instances, as nobly died, not only for "the honor of Connecticut," but for the honor and the rights of their entire race. This post of danger was too holy for Israel Putnam to take comfort in; and as he abandoned it, and those who were standing there, in June, 1775, so those who are his disciples and imitators, in 1859, assume to be as ignorant of its existence, and of the names of those who fought there, as they are ignorant, in reality, of the virtues, the bravery, the honor, and the patriotism of Thomas Knowlton, John Chester, William Coit, and their associates, from Connecticut, who stood behind the homely structure and battled with the enemy.

IV. Respecting the Horse-neck affair, so completely has it been exposed that I need not occupy your space further than by citing the words of Mr. Lossing (*Field Book of the Revolution*, 1 p. 413), who, after describing the ground, and giving a view of it, says: "The feat was perilous, but, under the circumstances, NOT VERY EXTRAORDINARY;" and by appealing to every person who has seen the side hill over which the General took his zig-zag sliding course, respecting the ENTIRE truth of Mr. Lossing's statement.

V. To my denial that "as the battle alarm came on the winds from Lexington, General Putnam left the plough in the furrow and hastened to the field of strife," &c., "*Selah*" interposes Dr. Allen's *Biographical Dictionary*. As an essential modification of this story, allow me to refer the attention of my opponent to *Bancroft's United States*, 7 pp. 315.

VI. To my denial of General Putnam's "intense and unconquerable desire to serve his country," *Selah*" parades, in reply, Dr. Dwight's eulogy and *the General's epitaph!*

The "honor of Connecticut" must be greatly endangered when the CHARACTERS of her heroes have no other standard THAN THEIR OWN EPITAPHS. In this selection "*Selah*" has done well, and evinced his zeal for the honor of his State. A theologian and an epitaph! Let us see what the facts are. PUTNAM entered the service as Second Brigadier General of the *Connecticut* troops—WOOSTER and SPENCER, being his superiors in everything but dishonesty. Soon afterwards a skirmish took place on Noddle's Island, in which Colonel JOHN STARK, with some New Hampshire troops, and some unknown officer, with a party of Massachusetts troops, displayed great abilities and firmness. A reinforcement was afterwards sent from Cambridge to strengthen Colonel STARK, and Doctor JOSEPH WARREN and General PUTNAM accompanied them; but as there were no Connecticut troops among them, General PUTNAM possessed no authority, and exercised none. The first news of the skirmish reached the Congress while that body was consulting on the subject of the General officers; and his friends, ever ready to seize any little circumstance which might benefit their own clique, claimed the victory for *him*, and, by pushing the subject, secured his appointment as Major-General, before the *truth* could reach the Congress. This result caused great dissatisfaction in the army, and drove from it some of its most able officers—all of which this "Christian Patriot" was fully advised of—yet he not only retained his appointment, to the injury of his country's cause, but, when General WASHINGTON desired to retain *all* the commissions, in order that the Congress might be enabled to reconsider the appointments, *pro bono publico*, PUTNAM frustrated the design, by securing, *by sharp prac-*

tice, the commission which had been filled with his name. "*Selah*" may find other details of this affair in ROGER SHERMAN's *Letter to General Wooster,* ("*Phila., June* 23, 1775,") and General WASHINGTON's *Letter to the President of Congress,* ("*Camp at Cambridge,* 10*th July,* 1775.") Shortly afterwards, the Battle of Bunker Hill was fought, and, as has been seen, this patriotic officer, a second time, attempted to appropriate, to his own advantage, the honors which others had gained. As "*Selah*" has informed us, PUTNAM was subsequently sent to the city of New York; but with such *positive* instructions, that he could do but little harm. (*Orders and Instructions to Major-General Putnam, March* 29, 1776.") While there, however, he received into his family the daughter of Major MONCRIEFFE, the distinguished *British* engineer, then on duty at Staten Island. "Not long after, a flag of truce arrived from Staten Island, with letters from Major MONCRIEFFE, demanding her; for he now considered her as a prisoner. General WASHINGTON would not acquiesce in this demand, saying, 'She should remain as a hostage for her father's good behavior!' When General WASHINGTON refused to give her up, *the noble-minded Putnam,* as if it were by instinct, laid his hand on his sword, and, with a violent oath, swore that 'her father's request *should* be granted.'" The "noble-minded PUTNAM"—"*Selah's*" patriotic and Christian-like hero—notwithstanding his "sword" and his "violent oath," did not secure the *female spy* from General WASHINGTON's grasp: and if "*Selah*" desires to pursue the investigation he will find the details in DAVIS' "*Memoirs of Aaron Burr,* 1 pp. 86-90, and in the "*Memoirs of Mrs. Margaret Coghlan,* (*Daughter of the late Major Moncrieffe*), Edit. New York, 1794, pages 35-40." Passing thence, over PUTNAM's exploits in the action on Long Island, at Philadelphia, and in the Highlands of the Hudson, in all of which "*Selah*" needs some light, I need only allude to his refusal to send forward the troops, when General WASHINGTON ordered them, which resulted in the loss of the forts on the Delaware, and the occupation of Philadelphia in 1777; and to the action of General WASHINGTON, when an attempt was made in the Congress, in 1772, to send PUTNAM to Rhode Island, which called forth that letter from Valley Forge, March 6, 1778, in which, after referring to PUTNAM, the illustrious chief uses these words: "With such materials as I have, the work must go on; whether well or ill, is another matter. If, therefore, he and others are not laid aside, they must be placed where they can least injure the service."

An opportunity to "lay him aside" soon occurred. The Congress had been, before, compelled, by the "higher power" of public opinion—the *vox populi*—to order an investigation of the causes which led to the loss of the Forts Clinton and Montgomery, (*Journal of Congress, Nov. 28, 1777,*) and, soon afterwards, grave charges were made against his fidelity to his country. One of these (*Robert R. Livingston, to General Washington, "Manor of Livingston, 14 January, 1778,"*) contains these words: "Your Excellency is not ignorant of the extent of General PUTNAM's capacity and diligence; and, how well soever these may qualify him for the management of this work, a most important command, the prejudices to which *his imprudent lenity to the disaffected, and a too great intercourse with the enemy*, have given rise, have greatly injured his influence. How far the loss of Fort Montgomery, and the subsequent ravages of the enemy, are to be imputed to him,

I will not venture to say, as this will necessarily be determined by a Court of Inquiry, whose determinations I would not anticipate. Unfortunately for him, the current of popular opinions, in this and the neighboring States, and as far as I can learn, in the troops under his command, runs strongly against him." If " *Selah* " can find comfort in the answer which this serious charge elicited from General WASHINGTON, I shall take pleasure in comforting him. In his letter to Mr. LIVINGSTON, (" *Valley Forge,* 12 *March,* 1778,") after acknowledging the receipt of the above, the General says : " It has not been an easy matter to find a just pretense for removing an officer from his command, where his misconduct rather appears to result from want of capacity, than from any real intention of doing wrong ; and it is therefore, as you observe, to be lamented that he cannot see his own defects, and make an honorable retreat from a station in which he only exposes his own weakness. Proper measures are taking to carry on the inquiry into the loss of Fort Montgomery, agreeably to the directions of Congress ; and it is more than probable, from what I have heard, that the issue of that inquiry will afford just grounds for a removal of General P. But whether it does or not, the prejudices of all ranks in that quarter against him are so great, that he must, at all events, be prevented from returning." As General PUTNAM was directed to proceed to Connecticut, soon afterwards, on recruiting service, and subsequently, it is said, joined the church, it has not appeared necessary to pursue this branch of my investigation. His subsequent conduct, on the recommendation of Mr. WHITING—whose funeral sermon over the General's remains was the commencement of the controversy on the subject of the command at Bunker Hill—

has been endorsed to the public by Dr. DWIGHT, the General's tomb-stone, and "*Selah*"; and I am not disposed to disturb its repose.

VII. "*Selah*" appears to desire notoriety, and he boldly asks a question respecting my motives in making the remarks on General PUTNAM, which he condemns; and as boldly he answers it :

"Fools rush in where angels fear to tread,"

and "*Selah*" may yet live to learn that, for the motives which actuate men, they are not accountable to man. If it will gratify him, however, I may suggest that his answer is not correct. General PUTNAM was not a *Connecticut* man, but a *Massachusetts* man; and that, of itself, would prove his error. I beg to suggest, however, that General PUTNAM never presented any trait of character which New York had any necessity to "envy." While he was in command of this post, *there was no "enemy" in the country*, to whom the city could be "given up" by its Tory inhabitants, or any other power; and if it had not been so, General PUTNAM could have done but little. General CHARLES LEE, *subsequently a traitor*, had formed plans for the defense of the city; and when General PUTNAM succeeded him, the latter was so tied down by orders, that no change could be made, except with the general *consent of his Brigadiers and Engineers*, and then only in minor matters. (*Orders and Instructions to Major-General Putnam, March*, 29, 1776.) What does "*Selah*" suppose New York has occasion to "*envy*" in General PUTNAM, while the slopes of *Gowannus* are daily before her eyes, and the *Highlands* within two hours' ride of the homes of her inhabitants? Does "*Selah*" suppose that his hero's manœuvres at the former place were so attractive that PHILIP SCHUYLER, or RICHARD MONTGOMERY, ALEXANDER MCDOUGAL, or JOHN MORIN SCOTT, MARINUS WILLETT, or JOHN LAMB, JAMES CLINTON, or NICHOLAS HERKIMER, GEORGE CLINTON, or BENJAMIN TALLMADGE, ALEXANDER HAMILTON, or AARON BURR,* could not have produced a result quite as profitable to the country, under similar circumstances? or which of these officers could not have been quite as successful as PUTNAM was, in his defense of the Highlands, Oct. 6, 1777?

In conclusion, I beg to remark that "*Selah*" manifests great uneasiness respecting the "honor of Connecticut," and "the Connecticut troops"—as much so, in fact, as if General PUTNAM was a Connecticut man; the only source of the honor of Connecticut; or the only soldier she ever produced. I beg "*Selah*" will keep perfectly cool. My business has not been, and is not now, with Connecticut men, the honor of Connecticut, or the troops she sent to the field. All these need no eulogy either from "*Selah*" or from me; nor can the detraction of either the one or the other seriously affect them. I have been, and still am, dealing SOLELY with a MASSACHUSETTS MAN, known as General ISRAEL PUTNAM, and a nondescript known as

---

* Colonel BURR, the least popular of these officers, was an aid-de-camp in General PUTNAM's family in 1776; and Colonel RICHARD PLATT, a distinguished officer of the Revolutionary army, thus compares the services of both these officers: "From my knowledge of that General's qualities and the Colonel's, *I am very certain that the latter directed all the movements and operations of the former.*"—(*Letter to Commodore Valentine Morris, New York, Jan. 27, 1814.*) In the same letter the same officer "presents BURR in contrast with his equals in rank, and his superiors in command," by comparing General PUTNAM's defeat in the Highlands, with two thousand men under his command, and Colonel BURR's successful movement, with one hundred and fifty men, in defending the west side of the river, below the Highlands, against the same enemy. The entire letter can be found in DAVIS' *Memoirs of Aaron Burr*, (N. Y., 1838) I pp. 175-181.

"*Selah.*" The former, by intrigues, and possibly by *bad liquor* dispensed over his own counter,* supplanted sundry Connecticut officers, whose services could be but poorly spared in exchange for his; did more than all others to disgrace Connecticut by his official incompetency, and by his selfish desire for the emoluments of office; and, by his disregard for every "generous impulse" which springs spontaneously from every honest man's breast, STOLE, for his own purposes, the glory which belonged to other and better men: the latter by a process peculiarly his own, seeks to keep the bubble inflated, and to conceal the deception which has so long been practised on the people. The former of these has gone to his reward: the latter, in the name of the mass of "the people of Connecticut," but without their authority, elevates "the relics" of his saint, and seeks the homage of the world. It has been my lot to refuse obedience to this demand; and if, in my humble endeavors to defend myself, I have been instrumental in drawing the attention of any to the evidences of the fraud; or if the memory of THOMAS KNOWLTON and his gallant associates has awakened a single sympathetic sigh, my labors have not been spent without a full and satisfactory reward.

Sincerely, Yours,
HENRY B. DAWSON.

---

* General PUTNAM, before he entered the service, *had kept a country tavern*, in the town of Pomfret. My readers, whether in Connecticut or New York, will recognize in the evil practice referred to in the text, one of the most usual and influential, but disreputable means by which ambitious and unscrupulous office-seekers, *such as Putnam was*, have ever endeavored to secure the votes which their own lack of merit could never command.

"SELAH'S" THIRD LETTER.

[FROM THE "HARTFORD DAILY POST," APRIL 18, 19, 20, 21, 23, 25, 1859.]

> " So prove it.
> That the probation bear no hinge nor loop,
> To hang a doubt on."

To the Editor of the Hartford Post:

In your issue for the 23d of February, appeared an article from my pen, "In Reply to Mr. DAWSON," which was called out by statements made by that gentleman, in a previous issue of your paper, in reference to the Life and Services of General PUTNAM. To this article Mr. DAWSON made reply in your issues for March 11 and 12, wherein he attempts to establish his statements by publishing an interminable list of references to "private letters," and in which also he does General PUTNAM the great injustice of adding still more epithets and inuendoes to the already long list which he had previously attached to the name and memory of that hero, both in his published work and in his former letters in your columns.

To refute these unjust and calumnious statements has been my great desire, since reading his last letter; but, through a great lack of time on my part, and also through the crowded state of your columns, for the past two or three weeks, I have been unable to fulfill the promise I had made myself, of giving to the public a few facts in regard to this affair, and showing them how little of impartial history lies in Mr. DAWSON's sketch of General PUTNAM's life.

In my former article, I substantiated the various deeds of honor and renown appertaining to General PUTNAM by such authorities as Dr. ALLEN, Dr. GRISWOLD, Colonel HUMPHREY, Dr. DWIGHT, Rev. Dr. WHITNEY, M. BOTTA, and Mr. BARBER—all of whom rank high in historical literature, and have been oft quoted as undoubted authorities. Mr. DAWSON, however, affects to laugh at them; casts them aside as worthless trash; claims them to be without authority; sets himself up, with his budget of "private letters," as the great "historical touchstone;" and, with all the complacence in the world, reels off seven mortal long columns, in the commendable purpose of giving the public a startling array of letter "titles," written, *perhaps*, by some one, and, *perhaps*, at some time, now to be found, *perhaps*, somewhere—where, probably Mr. DAWSON knows far better than any one else. Suffice it for my purpose to use one of these much vaunted "private letter" authorities as a test for the whole. I have had a note handed me within a few days, from a gentleman of this city, who had read Mr. DAWSON's letter, from which I was requested "to insert, in my next article," the following pertinent extract, with which request I take a particular pleasure in complying. Here we have it:—"A gentleman of this city will give ten dollars for a *duly authenticated* copy of the letter from Governor TRUMBULL, of Connecticut, to VAN DER CAPELLAN, in which the *former* informs the *latter* that *General Putnam did not command at Bunker's Hill!*" That is certainly fair enough; all that is required is a "*duly authenticated* copy" of the letter, to be deposited in the hands of the Secretary of this State, in this city, and the money will be forthcoming. It will *pay* Mr. DAWSON to copy that letter, and forward the same. He claimed, in his last, that Governor TRUMBULL wrote to JOHN DERK, Baron VAN DER CAPELLAN, that "General PUTNAM did not command at Bunker's Hill." If that letter is in existence, Mr. DAWSON can establish his authorities; otherwise they all fall to the ground.

Mr. DAWSON, in referring to the exploits of PUTNAM in the wolf-den, at Horseneck, and in the French War, adduces nothing to refute them that has a semblance of validity or argument. In fact, what he does say in regard to them is simply an acknowledgment of his performance of those daring feats, but a denial of there being any special merit or bravery in their performance. His sole object seems to be to detract from General PUTNAM's reputation as a man, a soldier, and a patriot. And in this endeavor he has touched most severely on his actions in the Battle of Bunker's Hill. Now, it is on the part he took in that battle that I would form a test. And it is also with the evidence that I will adduce in reference to General PUTNAM's position in that battle that I will build up at once a monument of that hero's glory and of Mr. DAWSON's shame.

And first, in regard to the part taken by General PUTNAM in the occupation of the heights of Bunker's Hill and the construction of the redoubts.

It is a well known fact that PUTNAM held a regularly commissioned command of the Continental troops previous to the battle of Bunker's Hill. The official certificate of

Mr. DAY, Secretary of the State of Connecticut, still on record, states that PUTNAM was appointed Brigadier-General over the forces of that colony, by the General Assembly, in April, 1775. He went to Cambridge immediately after the battle of Lexington, (*Notes to Colonel Swett's " History of the Bunker's Hill Battle,"* p. 20.) On the 27th of April, 1775, Colonel HUNTINGTON, of the Connecticut troop, wrote Governor TRUMBULL, from Cambridge, (*Massachusetts Historical Library*,) " General WARD being at Roxbury, General PUTNAM is commander-in-chief at this place." The Journal kept by Governor TRUMBULL, (*Trumbull Papers, Mass. Hist. Lib.*,) states that PUTNAM, "after learning of the battle of Lexington, rode over to him [the Governor] for instructions; and that he [the Governor] bade him " repair at once to Cambridge, and take charge of the troops, and he would make out his commission and send it on after him." Thus we have abundant evidence that General PUTNAM was the commander-in-chief of the American troops before the battle. Now, taking this for granted, it is but fair to suppose that he also commanded them in the battle.

When the subject of fortifying the heights of Bunker's Hill was first discussed in the American camp, the respective capabilities of the raw militia of the Colonies and the well-disciplined royal army were, of course, much canvassed, and many objections were raised as to the feasibility of a project which certainly seemed to promise a poor result to the brave but ill-disciplined militia, in their proposed passage at arms with a large force of royal troops, who, both officers and men, formed a selected section from Britain's military arm. General WARD and Dr. WARREN, both brave and gallant men, saw only destruction in the movement. Not so PUTNAM; he had served many long years, side by side, with Britain's cohorts, and knew that, though brave and efficient, they were not invincible. When WARD and WARREN made objection that the enterprise would lead to a general engagement, PUTNAM answered, (related by the General himself to his son, after the battle,) "We will risk only two thousand men; we will go on with these, and defend ourselves as long as possible; and, if driven to retreat, we are more active than the enemy, *and every stone-wall shall be lined with their dead!* and, at the worst, suppose us surrounded, and no retreat, *we will set our country an example of which it shall not be ashamed, and teach mercenaries what men can do determined to live or die free!*" Dr. WARREN walked the floor—leaned on his chair: "Almost thou persuadest me, General PUTNAM," said he; "but I must still think the project rash; if *you* execute it, however, you will not be surprised to find me by your side." "I hope not," responded General PUTNAM; "you are young, and your country has much to hope from you, in council and in the field; let us, who are old, and can be spared, begin the fray; there will be time enough for you hereafter; it will not soon be over!"

The primary object of fortifying Bunker's Hill, [or, more properly, Breed's Hill, on which the battle was fought, although it was a part of PUTNAM's plan to throw up earthworks on Bunker's Hill also, so that, in case of being driven from Breed's Hill by the enemy, they might make another stand on Bunker's Hill,] was to draw the enemy out of Boston, on ground where they might be met on equal terms. It was PUTNAM's favorite plan to erect breastworks on these heights, for, said he, (as reported by Governor BROOKS, of Massachusetts,) "The Americans were not afraid of their heads, though very much afraid of their legs; if you cover these, they will fight for ever."

On the 16th of June, 1775, " General PUTNAM (*Col. Swett,* p. 19,) having the principal direction and superintendence of the expedition, and the chief engineer, Colonel GRIDLEY, accompanied the detachment on to the heights," where, during the ensuing night, earthworks were thrown up with surprising rapidity, and of which the enemy knew nothing until the following morning. After PUTNAM had seen " the men quietly at their labors," (*Col. Swett,* p. 21,) he " repaired to his camp, to prepare for the anticipated crisis, by bringing on reinforcements and to be fresh mounted—his furious riding requiring a frequent change of horses." After performing these duties, " General PUTNAM, (*Frothingham's Siege of Boston,* p. 134,) *who had the confidence of the whole army,* again rode on to the heights, with the intention of remaining. to share their labors and perils!"

Still further, in reference to this part of the affair, we have evidence of the most reliable nature from Dr. STILES, afterwards President of Yale College, as noted down by him at the time, in his diary, and from which we will give the following extracts:—

" June 18th, 1775.—Nine o'clock this evening, a gentleman came to town from the camp, which he left this morning, and informs us that Colonel PUTNAM is encamped at Charlestown, Bunker's Hill, and has lost some of his best men, but is determined to stand his ground, having men enough.

" June 19th, 1775.—We have various accounts: some that General PUTNAM is taken and surrounded by the King's troops, some that he repulsed them, and had, by the assistance of others coming up, placed the regulars between two fires. At nine o'clock at night, the news was that General PUTNAM was forced from his trenches on Bunker's Hill, and obliged to retreat, with the loss of forty men killed and a hundred wounded.

"June 20th, 1775.—Mr. WILLIAM ELLERY came in, last evening, from Providence, and showed me a letter from the Chamber of Supplies, and another from General GREENE, to Lieutenant-Governor COOKE, (both at Roxbury,) dated on Lord's day, giving an account of the battle. General GREENE says, 'General PUTNAM, with three hundred men, took possession and entrenched on Bunker's Hill on Friday night, 16th instant;' the Chamber of Supplies says, 'The King's troops attacked General PUTNAM, who defended himself with bravery, till overpowered and obliged to retreat.'"

Judge GROSVENOR, of Pomfret, Connecticut, states, in an affidavit, that "he was in the Connecticut regiment," who, with "a much larger number of Massachusetts troops, under Colonel PRESCOTT, were ordered by General PUTNAM to march, on the evening of the 16th of June, 1775, to Breed's Hill, where, *under the immediate superintendence of General Putnam*, ground was broken, and a redoubt was formed."

We have also the words of Rev. Mr. WHITNEY, the personal friend and intimate acquaintance of PUTNAM, who says, "The detachment was first put under the command of General PUTNAM. With it he took possession of the hill, and ordered the battle from beginning to end. These facts General PUTNAM gave me soon after the battle, and also repeated them to me after his Life was printed." [His Life, by Colonel HUMPHREY, Mr. WHITNEY refers to. Colonel HUMPHREY's "Life of PUTNAM" was published when the General was still alive. It was written at Mount

Vernon, without any communication with PUTNAM on the subject, and without his knowledge. It is not, therefore, remarkable that the Colonel should have erred in the single matter of commandership, where he assigns to his hero everything else that is great and honorable.]

We have, still further, Major DANIEL JACKSON'S entry in his Journal, dated June 16, 1775, where he says, "General PUTNAM, with the army, went to entrench on Bunker's Hill." And JOHN BOYLE, who also kept a diary at that time, and entered therein, under date June 16, 1775, "General PUTNAM, with a detachment of about one thousand of American forces, went from Cambridge, and began an entrenchment on an eminence below Boston." And, most reliable evidence, an extract from RIVINGTON'S "New York Gazette," for 3d of August, 1775, stating that "PUTNAM, on the evening of the 16th of June, took possession of Bunker's Hill, and began an entrenchment."

Thus it seems to be conclusively proven that the detachment went on to the heights under the command of General PUTNAM, and began there those entrenchments which were to serve so good a purpose on the following day. It is vouched for by such witnesses and documents as the above, all of whom agree in the main point of who commanded, and differ only in the simple matter of the numbers composing the detachment taken on to the field, which, under the circumstances, is not to be wondered at.

When the morn broke upon the heights of Bunker's and Breed's Hills, and upon the shipping in the harbor, and the town of Boston, what was the amazement of the British at seeing those heights covered with earthworks and alive with continental troops—all the work of one night, as if wrought by the hand of some powerful genii. The British ships immediately opened their fire upon the redoubts, as did also batteries lining the wharves in Boston. How high must have beat the mingling hopes and fears of those brave men, on those imperiled heights, upon whom all-powerful Britain was soon to unleash and hound " the dogs of war." They had worked almost miracles during the season of darkness that had just passed; but there was much left undone, through sheer want of time and men, and on the completion of which depended, to a great extent, the success of the enterprise. The commanding summit of Bunker's Hill, of vital importance, in case of a retreat, was not yet fortified, " though PUTNAM," (says *Col. Swett*, p. 28,) " mortified at the neglect of a position on which *his success and reputation depended*, had been incessant and unwearied in his efforts to have it accomplished; but in vain, as no reinforcements arrived."

" On seeing the preparations of the enemy for an attack," continues Colonel SWETT, " General PUTNAM again hastened to Cambridge for reinforcements, and had to pass through a galling, enfilading fire of round, bar, and chain-shot, which thundered across the Neck, from the *Glasgow* frigate, in the channel of Charles River, and two floating batteries hauled close to the shore." He, on arriving at Cambridge, learned from General WARD the orders which had been sent to the New Hampshire troops at Medford, and immediately returned to his post on the field of battle. This New Hampshire regiment, under Colonel STARK, arrived on the field between two and three o'clock in the afternoon, and " General PUTNAM (*Frothingham*, p. 134,) ordered part of them to labor on the works begun on Bunker's Hill, and part to the redoubts."

" PUTNAM was now joined (*Col. Swett*, p. 31,) by Dr.

Warren, to whom he observed, 'I'm sorry to see you here, General Warren. I wish you had left the day to us, as I advised you. From appearances, we shall have a sharp time of it; but, since you are here, I'll receive your orders with pleasure.'* Warren replied, 'I came only as a volunteer; *I know nothing of your dispositions,* and will not interfere with them. Tell me where I can be most useful!' Putnam, intent on his safety, directed him to the redoubt, observing, 'You will be covered there.' 'Don't think,' said Warren, 'I came here to seek a place of safety; but tell me where the onset will be most furious.' Putnam again pointed to the redoubt: 'That,' said he, 'is the enemy's object; Prescott is there, and will do his duty, and if it can be defended, the day is ours; but from long experience of the character of the enemy, I think they will ultimately succeed, and drive us from the works; though, from the mode of attack they have chosen, we shall be able to do them infinite injury; and we must be prepared for a brave and orderly retreat, when we can maintain our ground no longer!'"

As soon as the British lines came into full view to the Americans, and within musket range, it was with great difficulty that Putnam could restrain his men, especially the good marksmen, from firing upon them. "He rode through the lines," (*says Col. Swett*, p. 33,) "and ordered

---

* "*Selah*" would have done well had he explained *why* the "commander-in-chief of the American troops before the battle" (*vide page* 67) offered to "receive" Warren's "orders with pleasure," as here stated. Was it because the military abilities of this Boston physician, a mere novice in military affairs, were superior to his own; or did he suppose General Warren—a Major-General in the Massachusetts militia, without his commission—had ranked him? A pretty "commander-in-chief of the American troops," in either case, was such an officer. H. B. D.

that no one should fire till the enemy were within eight rods of the breastworks; nor any one then even, until he had given the word. 'Powder,' said PUTNAM, 'was scarce, and must not be wasted. They should not fire at the enemy till they saw the whites of their eyes, and then fire low; take aim at their waistbands. They were all marksmen, and could kill a squirrel at a hundred yards; reserve their fire, and the enemy were all destroyed. Aim at the handsome coats; pick off the commanders.'"

"PUTNAM now," (*says Col. Swett,*) "with the assistance of Captain FORD's company, opened his artillery upon them. He had on this day performed every species of service, and now turned cannonier, with splendid success, and to the highest satisfaction of his countrymen. He pointed the cannon himself, the balls took effect on the enemy, and one case of cannister made a lane through them!"

On came the British columns, in close order, with most martial appearance and imposing array. On, on they came, the glory of war kindling in their eyes, and vengeance breathing from their lips, at the "cursed rebels," who had thus "dared" to beard the lion in his den. On, on they came, until the breastworks were almost gained, and hopes of an easy and speedy victory swelled their bosoms. On they came, till the "whites of their eyes" were seen by those firm, dauntless, almost breathless militia men; and then there was a fearful lowering of those "deadly tubes," a keen glance along their shining sides—a moment of breathless suspense—a deep, full word of command—a vivid flash and a sullen roar, as from heaven's artillery—quick successive volleys, each following each more dreadful than the former; and, above all the din of this awful battery, rose the shrieks and wails of the wounded and dying! Nothing of mortal make could withstand this awful tide of fire and death! They faltered—they wavered—they broke, and fled adown the hill. Down that hill, up whose verdant sides they had but just swept, a glorious sight, in their pride and confidence, in their pomp of equipage and their glory of strength and invincibility!

It was after this first retreat of the enemy that General WARD dispatched re-enforcements from Cambridge to the field of strife. But the fire from the British ships, across the Neck, over which they would have to pass, was now so terrific that, raw recruits as they were, they wavered in the attempt. "PUTNAM," (*says Col. Swett*, p. 35,) "flew to the spot to overcome their fears, and hurry them on before the enemy returned. He entreated, encouraged and threatened them; lashing his horse with the flat of his sword, he rode backward and forward across the Neck; the balls threw up clouds of dust around him, and the soldiers were perfectly convinced that *he* was invulnerable, but were not equally conscious of being so themselves." Some of these troops, however, ventured over. It was while on his return from the Neck, that General PUTNAM came upon Colonel GERRISH and his regiment—the Colonel GERRISH whom General DEARBORN, and Mr. DAWSON after him, have converted into such a large sized bug-bear. Colonel GERRISH confessed to General PUTNAM that he was very much exhausted, owing to his great corpulency and the fatigues of his late march. "General PUTNAM," (*says Frothingham*, page 143,) "endeavored to rally these troops. He used entreaty and command, and offered to lead them into action, but without effect." They were in a most complete state of insubordination, arising from the condition of their commander, and their not having had previous knowledge of the rank of General PUTNAM, and consequently doubting his authority.

Much confusion prevailed in other sections of the troops, arising principally from the lax discipline of the men—the insufficient number of officers, many of whom knew little or nothing of the duties assigned them—the impromptu nature of the whole affair, and the consequent want of that thorough study of the plan of the battle, and the requisite conforming of means and material to the circumstances; and, sorest want of all, an inadequate supply of ammunition, much of which, too, was unfitted for the purposes for which it was intended, inasmuch as many of the cartridges for the field-pieces were too large. Colonel SWETT tells us that PUTNAM, observing that some of the field-pieces had ceased their fire, inquired the cause, when they gave the reason of their inability to load the guns with the cartridges, they being too large. Upon which "PUTNAM broke open the cartridges, and loaded the guns with a *ladle*, and sighted and fired them several times himself."

"The artillery companies, under CALLENDER and GRIDLEY, (*says Col Swett*, pp. 29, 30,) "were just enlisted from the infantry, and grossly ignorant of their duty." He goes on to say that GRIDLEY drew off his company, with their pieces, to the rear; "and CALLENDER was marching off over Bunker's Hill, to secure a place for preparing his ammunition in safety, when PUTNAM met him, and was fired with indignation at this appearance of a retreat. He ordered him instantly to his post; CALLENDER remonstrated; but PUTNAM threatened him with instant death if he hesitated, and compelled him to return." The above is-also verified by a Report made to the Massachusetts Provincial Congress, in 1775, in which it is stated that, on the day of the battle, "PUTNAM met Captain CALLENDER, of the artillery, retreating down the hill; PUTNAM ordered him 'to stop and go back.'"

In the meantime, the British had formed anew, at the bottom of the hill, and once more were marching up, over the bodies of their fallen comrades, into the very face of those terrible marksmen. True, they came not, this time, with that show of conscious and undoubted strength, and that triumphant flash in their eyes; but on they came, with a look of determination—the determination which speaks either of death or victory. Again were they met by that murderous fire, opening upon them from the whole American line, and again they wavered, turned and fled. Indomitable and unyielding, in their scorn of the idea of defeat, as well as their deep desire to mete out revenge upon the slayers of their comrades, again they form, again return to the fray, and effect a lodgment within the works of the Americans. The ammunition of the Americans had failed. There was not the means wherewith to pour in that awful fire upon the advancing columns for the third time. They clubbed their muskets, and with nerves of iron and feelings of deep, unutterable despair, dealt blows, thick and powerful, upon the invaders of their country and their country's rights. But alas! what are clubbed muskets when arrayed against British bayonets? Nothing. There was but one thing to be done—and that, to retreat.

Even when the Americans were driven from the breastworks, and forced to retreat, the British lines were not in much better condition. They were entirely exhausted by their desperate efforts, under a blazing sun, and were dreadfully broken by the well-directed fire of the Americans. To such an extent were their ranks broken and confused, that their right and left wings were facing each other, with the Americans between; thus would their fire have slain alike friend and foe. While they endeavored to form anew, the Americans also collected, and made a brave and orderly retreat. At this juncture, "PUTNAM," (*says Col. Swett*, p. 46,) "put spurs to his foaming horse, and threw himself between the retreating force and the enemy, who were but twelve rods from him. His countrymen were in momentary expectation of seeing this compeer of the immortal WARREN fall. He entreated them to rally, and renew the fight—to finish his works on Bunker's Hill—and again give the enemy battle on that unassailable position, and pledged his honor to restore to them an easy victory."

"During the retreat," (*says Frothingham*, p. 152,) "which, for the most part, lay over the brow of Bunker's Hill, where was the place of the greatest slaughter, General PUTNAM rode to the rear of the retreating troops, and, regardless of the balls flying about him, with his sword drawn, and still undaunted in his bearing, urged them to renew the fight in the unfinished works." "Make a stand here," he exclaimed, (*Frothingham*, p. 152; also *affidavits of Col. Wade, Major Elihu Lyman, and Anderson Miner*,) "we can stop them yet. In God's name, form, and give them one shot more!" "The enemy pressed on them, and they were, in turn, compelled to retire. PUTNAM covered their retreat with his Connecticut troops, and others just arrived; and, in the rear of the whole, dared the utmost fury of the enemy, who pursued with little ardor, but poured in their thundering volleys, and showers of balls fell like hail around the General. He addressed himself to every passion of the troops, to persuade them to rally, to throw up his works on Bunker's Hill, and make a stand there; and threatened them with the eternal disgrace of deserting their General! He took his stand near a fieldpiece, and seemed resolved to brave the foe alone. His troops, however, felt it impossible to withstand the overwhelming force of the British bayonets; they left him. One sergeant alone dared to stand by his General to the last. He was shot down; and the enemy's bayonets were just upon the General when he retired." (*Frothingham*, p. 152; *Col. Swett*, p. 47: also *Affidavits of Gov. Brooks, Col. Wade, Judge Grosvenor, Maj. Elihu Lyman, Col. Webb, Anderson Miner, Joshua Yeomans, Simeon Noyes*, and many others.)

Thus have I followed up the authorities bearing upon this subject, from the first planning of the battle at Cambridge, through the awful strife that followed, and the retreat of the Americans over Charlestown Neck, back to their camp at Cambridge. There is no one particular point or action, in reference to the whole affair, in which we do not find PUTNAM participating, and even leading the way. History has mingled his name with the relation of every salient point in that fearful conflict. In addition to the mass of authorities already given, we find Judge GROSVENOR stating that "PUTNAM ordered KNOWLTON to his position;" Judge WINTHROP's statement, in an article in the "North American Review," for July, 1818, that he "saw PUTNAM here [Breed's Hill] just previous to the first attack;" and SIMEON NOYES, taking oath, in an affidavit in 1825, that "PUTNAM rode up to the company he was in, and said: 'Draw off your troops here,' pointing to the rail-fence, 'for the enemy's flanking us fast.'"

We have, too, from a letter written by Colonel SAMUEL WARD, of Rhode Island, under date 20th of June, 1775, the statement that "PUTNAM had a sore battle on Saturday." ETHAN CLARK writes to Colonel WARD, "We hear that PUTNAM is defeated, and Dr. WARREN slain." Dr. AARON DEXTER, in a statement written out from memoranda, made by himself at the time, and by him preserved, says, "The day after the battle, I was at General WARD's quarters, and was informed by the officers there that General PUTNAM had command of all the troops which were sent down over night, and which might be ordered there the next day." Captain TREVETT, senior captain of artillery, acting under Major GRIDLEY, who had chief command of the artillery on that day, (*Col. Swett*, p. 21,) inquired officially of the Major "who had command of the troops?" and was informed by him that "General PUTNAM had;" upon which Captain TREVETT remarked, "Then there is nothing to fear," and immediately applied to PUTNAM for orders, and received them. And WILLIAM WILLIAMS, the son-in-law of Governor TRUMBULL, and a member of the Continental Congress at Philadelphia, in a letter addressed to that body, under date "Lebanon, Connecticut, June 20th, 1775, 10 o'clock at night," says, "I receive it that General PUTNAM commanded our troops; perhaps not in chief."*

I have oftentimes wondered how any man can be so perfectly devoid of all common reasoning as to accept the blind and scandalous statements of General DEARBORN,

---

* As General PUTNAM *was* the commander of "*our*"—THE CONNECTICUT—"*troops*," Mr. WILLIAMS' supposition was nearer correct than "SELAH'S" assertion; but why my opponent added the last paragraph, which so pointedly discredits his theory respecting the chief command, is beyond my comprehension.   H. B. D.

when there is lying in every historical collection so much that gives his statements such a strong coloring of untruth. I can go to many, many places to find evidence, in the original, of all that has been claimed in PUTNAM's favor, but know not where (aside from DEARBORN's assertions, and their reproduction by others, who have either ignorantly or maliciously accepted them as truth,) I could go to procure evidence of "vileness," "cowardice," "insufficiency, or criminality," in that hero.

Among all the evidences of the part taken by PUTNAM in the Bunker's Hill battle, no insignificant one may be found in a colored portrait, on paper, of the General, published by " C. SHEPHERD, Sept., 1775," *only three months after the battle,* which bears on its margin the following words: " ISRAEL PUTNAM, Esq., Major-General of the Connecticut forces, and commander-in-chief at the engagement on Bunker's Hill, near Boston, 17th of June, 1775." This picture is in this city, and has been seen by many of our citizens.

Dr. JAMES THATCHER, in his "Military Journal," says that " on the American side, Generals PUTNAM, WARREN, POMEROY, and Colonel PRESCOTT, were emphatically the heroes of the day, and their unexampled efforts were crowned with glory." In this extract it will be seen that THATCHER places the name of PUTNAM first, thus seeming to give him precedence also in command.

We even have the evidence and testimony of the British in reference to this matter, and all of which goes to establish PUTNAM's claims to the honor, not only of commandership, but of having taken a brave and daring part in the strife. From a letter written by a British officer, in the army in Boston, to a friend in England, dated June 25th,

1775. and which may be found in the "American Archives," vol. II., p. 1093, we quote the two following passages: "After the skirmish of the 17th, we even commended the troops of *Putnam*, who fought so gallantly, *pro aris et focis*." And again, "So very secret was the late action conducted, that Generals CLINTON and BURGOYNE knew not of it till the morning; though the town did in general, and *Putnam* in particular." Colonel ABERCROMBIE, who commanded the British grenadiers, was killed in the engagement. "He had been a personal friend and a warm one," (*says Col. Swett*, p. 42,) "to General PUTNAM in bygone days." And, continues SWETT, "So dear was PUTNAM to him as a soldier, patriot and friend, that, dying, he remembered him, and enjoined it on his countrymen, who surrounded him, 'If you take General PUTNAM alive, don't hang him; for he is a brave fellow!'"

It will be noticed that I have made frequent reference to Colonel SWETT's work, the "Account of the Bunker's Hill Battle." I have taken him to be as good and impartial authority in this case as can be obtained, for several reasons. Colonel SWETT was in the staff of Governor BROOKS, of Massachusetts, and enjoyed his friendship to an extraordinary degree. Consequently he received the Governor's hearty co-operation and aid in the compilation of his work. The battle was probably never understood by any one better than by Governor BROOKS. "He was with the troops on the battle-field," (*says Col. Swett,*) "from the first to the last; and certainly enjoyed an extraordinary opportunity of gathering information, which, joined to a deep desire to inquire at the time, and ever after, into the occurrences, allowed of no chance for aught of importance to escape him." Colonel SWETT, in his work, gives some sixty affidavits, taken before magistrates and others, all conferring on PUTNAM the honor of commanding the troops in the battle, and also of taking a brave and noble part throughout the contest. These affidavits were taken, many of them, at the instance of Colonel SWETT, and *may all of them be relied on.* FROTHINGHAM says of them that they "are statements chiefly taken by Colonel SWETT, *whose high sense of honor is a guaranty of their fidelity !*"

Depositions were taken (which depositions are preserved) from the following individuals, all of whom were men in high standing for truth, and whose credibility was never impeached—men, too, who had ample means of knowing what they swore to, inasmuch as they all were either on or near the battle-field on the day of the action. Among these men were JOSIAH CLEVELAND, of Canterbury, Connecticut, in PUTNAM's regiment; JOSHUA YEOMANS, of Norwich, also in PUTNAM's regiment; Governor BROOKS, of Massachusetts, in the action; Judge GROSVENOR, of Pomfret, Connecticut, in the action; ABNER ALLEN, of Western, in the action; JOSIAH HILL, of Tyringham, in PUTNAM's regiment; the Rev. Army Chaplain; THOMAS COOKE, Esq., member of the Massachusetts Congress, and a signer of "*Sword in hand money;*" REUBEN KEMP, of Brooklyn, Connecticut, one of Colonel STARK's men; ISAAC BASSETT, of Killingly, in PUTNAM's regiment; EBENEZER BEAN, of Conway, in STARK's regiment; Judge Advocate TUDOR; President ADAMS, Sen.; Captain JOHN BARKER, of Pomfret, Connecticut, in REED's New Hampshire regiment; Major ELIHU LYMAN, of Greenfield, a lieutenant in the battle; ANDERSON MINER, in Major Lyman's company; General KEYS, for many years Adjutant General of Connecticut, and who served in the battle, as a first lieutenant in PUT-

NAM's regiment; ABIEL BUGBEE, of Pomfret, Connecticut, in PUTNAM's regiment; JOHN DEXTER, of Pomfret, Vermont, in PUTNAM's regiment; ALEXANDER DAVIDSON, of Edgecombe, in FORD's company; Colonel EBENEZER BANCROFT, Esq., of Tyngsborough, a captain in BRIDGE's regiment; Captain JAMES CLARK, who commanded one hundred men in PUTNAM's regiment; Major JOHN BURNHAM, of Londonderry, a lieutenant in LITTLE's regiment; Colonel PUTNAM, a son of the General, who was in his father's regiment; General PEIRCE, of Hillsborough, in FORD's company; RICHARD GILCHRIST, of Dublin, in STARK's regiment; BENJAMIN MANN, a captain in REED's regiment; ISRAEL HUNT, of Dunstable, in BRIDGE's regiment; JOSEPH TRASK, of Billerica, in GARDNER's regiment; FRANCIS DAVIDSON, of Londonderry, in FORD's company; JOB SPAFFORD, of Berlin, a sergeant in General WARD's regiment; JESSE SMITH, of Salem, a private in the action: A. DICKERSON, of Amherst, in WOODBRIDGE's regiment; WILLIAM FRENCH, of Dunstable, a private, and one of those engaged in throwing up the redoubts; RUSSELL DEWEY, of Westfield, a private in the action; BENJAMIN BULLARD, of Hopkinton, a captain in BREWER's regiment; ENOS LAKE, of Ringe, in REED's regiment; WM. LOW, of Gloucester, in the action; PHILIP BAGLEY, in FRYE's regiment, and, after the war, a deputy-sheriff in the city of Newburyport for nearly thirty years; THOMAS DAVIS, of Holden, in the action; JOHN HOLDEN, of Leicester, in DOOLITTLE's regiment; SAMUEL JONES, of Sudbury, in DOOLITTLE's regiment; NATHANIEL RICE, of East Sudbury, in the action; SIMEON NOYES, of Salem, in LITTLE's regiment; WM. MARDEN, of Portsmouth, in GERRISH's regiment; AMOS FOSTER, of Tewksbury, in the action; Colonel WADE, of

Ipswich, a captain in LITTLE's regiment, and afterwards treasurer of Essex County, Massachusetts; JOHN STEVENS, of Andover, in FRYE's regiment; GEORGE LEACH, of Salem, in WHITCOMB's regiment; DAVID BREWER, of Framingham, in the action; ELIJAH JOURDAN, of Bucksfield, in the action; Colonel J. PAGE, of Atkinson, in the action; AARON SMITH, of Shrewsbury, in the action; EZRA RUNNELS, of Middleborough, in GRIDLEY's artillery company; Colonel JOSEPH WHITTEMORE, of Newburyport, a lieutenant in LITTLE's regiment; PHILIP JOHNSON, Esq., of Newburyport, in LITTLE's regiment; SAMUEL BASSETT, in STARK's regiment; Deacon MILLAR, of Charlestown, in GARDNER's regiment; ENOCH BALDWIN, of Milton, in GARDNER's regiment; Judge WINTHROP, in the action; JOHN HOPKINS, of Templeton, in GARDNER's regiment; Mr. THOMPSON, of Charlestown, in GARDNER's regiment; WM. DICKSON, of Charlestown, in GARDNER's regiment; Major DANIEL JACKSON, of Newton, in FOSTER's artillery company; Captain FRANCIS GREENE, of Boston, a sergeant in FOSTER's company, and, after the war, one of the assessors of the city of Boston.

These depositions were taken, some before Judges of the Supreme Court; some before "General SULLIVAN, and other Directors of the Bunker's Hill Monument Association, assisted by Judge THATCHER and others;" some before Colonel SAMUEL SWETT; some before Adjutant-General SUMNER; and others before WM. STEVENSON, Esq., of Canterbury, Connecticut; B. MERRILL, Esq., of Salem; SAMUEL F. BROWN, Esq., of Bucksfield; JOHN VOSE, Esq., of Atkinson; S. D. WARD, Esq., of Shrewsbury; WILKES WOOD, Esq., of Middleborough; Hon. EBENEZER MOSELEY, of Newburyport; and other highly respectable magistrates.

In their depositions they all agree that PUTNAM was on Bunker's and Breed's Hills, both on the night of the 16th and during the day of the 17th of June, 1775. They all agree, too, that he there performed the duties devolving upon a commander; and that they, as well as their comrades in arms, "always considered him their commander," on that day. They all agree as to his conduct on the battle-field on that occasion; and, in their affidavits, speak with a confidence and freedom that proclaims for them a thorough knowledge of what they speak of, and an honesty of purpose in their statements. They, in many cases, use words of the highest import in reference to the subject in hand; and I cannot deny myself the pleasure of giving a few quotations from these affidavits.

Governor BROOKS testifies to PUTNAM's daring and reckless bravery, when, with a sergeant only, he stood by the guns till the sergeant was shot down, and the British bayonets nearly pressed his own bosom ere he retreated. Judge GROSVENOR says that, "under the immediate superintendence of General PUTNAM, ground was broken and a redoubt was formed:" that "the General directed, principally, the operations of the succeeding day;" and that "*he inspired confidence by his example.*" Mr. ALLEN says that "he saw PUTNAM on horseback, urging the men to fight, with great earnestness. Mr. HILL says, "I know that General PUTNAM was in the battle, took part in the engagement, and was as much exposed as any one in the battle." Mr. COOKE, a member of the Massachusetts Congress, says that PUTNAM "did all that man could do to get on the men to Breed's Hill; he appeared firm, resolute, and thoughtless of personal danger; his praise was in the mouth of every one at that time; *he never heard a disre-*

spectful word against him!" Mr. KEMP says, "General PUTNAM seemed to have the ordering of things." Mr. BASSETT says, "I saw General PUTNAM in the hottest of the fight, calling on the men to stand their ground." Judge Advocate TUDOR, who presided at the court martial that followed the battle, says, "In the inquiry which those trials occasioned, *I never heard an insinuation against the conduct of General Putnam!*" President ADAMS, Senior, says, "This I do say, without reserve, *I never heard the least insinuation of dissatisfaction with the character of General Putnam during his whole life!*" Major ELIHU LYMAN says, "General PUTNAM was present directing the retreat, riding backward and forward *between us and the British*, and appeared cool and deliberate, frequently speaking to the men." Colonel BANCROFT, who served with PUTNAM in the old French war, says, "he had seen him often in the midst of danger; his courage could not be doubted, nor his character impeached." And, in reference to the Bunker's Hill affair, where he assisted in throwing up the redoubts, he says "The lines were marked out by PUTNAM." Mr. MINER "saw General PUTNAM riding through the American ranks, amidst showers of balls, undaunted, with his sword drawn, exhorting the troops, 'in the name of God,' to form and give the British one shot more, and then they might retreat." Mr. BURNHAM says that PUTNAM "appeared busily engaged in giving directions to the troops as they came up," and that the company to which he belonged received their orders from PUTNAM. Mr. YEOMANS states that he "was well acquainted with General PUTNAM; saw a great deal of him in the action, encouraging the men. He saw him ride along the whole line, and crying out, 'stick to your posts, men, and do your duty;' he was greatly exposed." Mr. BAGLEY "saw General PUTNAM pass up and down the line on horseback, during the battle, encouraging the soldiers. The shot were very thick where he was; he had a very calm, encouraging look. Knew him because I had seen him at Cambridge." Mr. JONES " saw General PUTNAM, and spoke with him ; he encouraged us very much, and rode up and down behind us; his horse was all of a lather, and the battle was going on very hotly at the time." Colonel WADE says of PUTNAM, "He was the only officer I saw on horseback. He seemed busily engaged in bringing on troops." Mr. JOURDAN says, " I perfectly well remember that General PUTNAM was in the entrenchment very frequently during the engagement, giving orders as commander-in-chief." Mr. SMITH says of PUTNAM, "He appeared to me to have, and I always understood he had, the command of the troops." Mr. JOHNSON states that, "just before the action began, he saw General PUTNAM on horseback, very near him, and distinctly heard him say, 'Men, you know you are all marksmen—you can take a squirrel from the tallest tree. Don't fire till you see the whites of their eyes.'" He again says that, " immediately after the first retreat of the British, General PUTNAM rode up and said, ' Men, you have done well, but next time you will do better ; aim at the officers.'" Colonel WHITMORE says that " on the retreat, he was wounded in the thigh ; he soon after saw General PUTNAM ; and well knowing the General, and the General knowing him, he said, ' General, shan't we rally again ?' to which PUTNAM replied, ' Yes, as soon as we can; are you wounded ?'" Mr. RICE says that he " saw PUTNAM riding round, encouraging the people to the utmost, both before the battle and during the battle." The

Rev. Army Chaplain, who makes a statement of facts, under oath, in reference to the gallant conduct of PUTNAM on the field of 17th of June, 1775, closes his deposition by stating that "he was the intimate friend of Colonel PRESCOTT and Lieutenant-Colonel ROBINSON, *and from the mouths of these heroes he had this account.*"

What a mass of testimony is here presented. Testimony, too, that may be relied on, coming, as it does, from men of the greatest respectability, and some of them in high stations in life, and all making their statements *under an oath*, "to tell the truth, the whole truth, and nothing but the truth." And what have General PUTNAM's detractors ever brought forward to rebut this mass of authority? Why, of all the evidence adduced by them at various times, and their affidavits, taken from persons sworn, as they claim, *only one* makes the assertion, bold and bare-faced, that General PUTNAM was not on the field, nor took any part in the battle; and he, in the intricate mazes of his own *fabricated* testimony, blunders and stumbles in a manner most pitiful, and at the same time most amusing.

In regard to the difficulty between Colonel PRESCOTT and General PUTNAM, out of which Mr. DAWSON has attempted to make a great deal of capital, I have searched the authorities in vain to find evidence of a *quarrel* between them. The only occurrence on which any one might find ground to build such a supposition, is in the simple fact that "General PUTNAM, (*Frothingham*, p. 129,) who was on his way to the heights when Major BROOKS was going to Cambridge, rode on horseback to the redoubt, and told Colonel PRESCOTT (*General Heath's Memoirs*, p. 19,) that the entrenching tools must be sent off, or they would be lost;

to which the Colonel replied, that, if he sent any of the men away with the tools, not one of them would return : to this the General answered. 'They shall every man return!' A large part of these tools were carried no farther than Bunker's Hill, where, by General PUTNAM's order, the men began to throw up a breastwork. Most of them fell into the hands of the enemy." How any one can twist the above conversation into a quarrel, I cannot conceive. The above facts are not only vouched for by the two eminent authorities mentioned in parenthesis, but also by a statement of Mr. JOSEPH PEARCE, in 1818, and by a MS. letter by Colonel EBENEZER BANCROFT, written December 7th, 1824.

General DEARBORN was the first to make the statement —which Mr. DAWSON has copied into his published work almost *verbatim*—that Colonel PRESCOTT, at a dinner given by Governor BOWDOIN, of Massachusetts, denounced General PUTNAM as "a self-conceited, inefficient man, and deserving to be shot." It is too late now to question whether PRESCOTT ever made use of these words, as in fact it was, even at the time that DEARBORN published his work—both PUTNAM and PRESCOTT then being in their graves. But it has most generally been regarded, by sober-thinking, sensible men, as a misconception—either intentional or otherwise—of Colonel PRESCOTT's true words and their meaning. Who can for a moment reconcile any such occurrence with the well-known fact that PRESCOTT and PUTNAM ever stood on the most friendly terms, the one with the other? How little weight may be attached to General DEARBORN's statements, in regard to the affairs of the Bunker's Hill battle, may be conceived, when it is known that the position held by himself in the battle was that of a platoon officer, commanding some twenty to thirty men, and was engaged, like them, in loading and discharging his musket. Any one may readily perceive that a man in that position could not possibly be familiar with the actions and conduct of a commanding officer, nor of anything that was transpiring in another quarter of the field from that in which he was posted. Yet he had the cool effrontery to write a work, purporting to be a correct mirror of that battle, and in it condemns and berates General PUTNAM in the most unjust and unkind manner, and has—oh! when will wonders cease?—won over adherents and disciples to his heresies, among whom Mr. DAWSON numbers himself.

When the court martial was held, after the battle, before which the cases of Colonel GERRISH, Captain CALLENDER, Colonel SCAMMANS, Lieutenant WOODWARD, Major GRIDLEY, and other officers, were tried on a charge of cowardice, a committee was appointed by Congress to inquire into the facts of the case. This committee reported that "They had made inquiry of General PUTNAM, and other officers, *who were in the hottest of the battle*, and that General PUTNAM charged Captain CALLENDER and another artillery officer with infamous cowardice—one of the principal causes of the defeat—and informed them that he would quit the service if these officers were not made an example of, and that one of them ought to be shot." How very like is the wording of the last sentence of this report of the committee of Congress to that sentence of condemnation which DEARBORN has made Colonel PRESCOTT utter against the character of General PUTNAM; and how very ikely is it, too, that the Colonel was referring to the same report of the committee, and using their language, with its same purport, which General DEARBORN, with eager pen, turned into a charge by the Colonel against PUTNAM himself.

Colonel SCAMMANS, soon after the trial, published a report in a newspaper, of the court martial held on himself, in which he stated that General PUTNAM was not engaged in the battle at all. And yet, it appears in evidence, during the trial, from witnesses under oath, that this very Colonel SCAMMANS, while the battle was going on, *sent his sergeant to General Putnam to see if he* (SCAMMANS) *was wanted!* and this very sergeant was in the court during the trial, and took oath *that such was the case.*

In a former letter by Mr. DAWSON, he attempts to throw over the connections of Colonel SMALL and Major MONCRIEF (both of the royal army) and General PUTNAM the coloring of duplicity and treason on the General's part; and goes so far as to say that, had not this connection been watched, and its results prevented, General PUTNAM would have proved another traitor ARNOLD! When the facts of this connection are thoroughly known, the deep injustice of this charge by Mr. DAWSON will be seen and duly appreciated. Colonel SMALL was intimately acquainted with General PUTNAM previous to the Battle of Bunker's Hill, having served with him during the war in Canada, from 1756 to 1763. Colonel JOHN TRUMBULL, the painter, and a son of Governor TRUMBULL, of this State, while painting a picture of the battle of Bunker's Hill, during a residence in London, in the summer of 1786, was visited at his studio one day by Colonel SMALL. The Colonel remarked to the painter, looking at the picture, "I don't like the situation in which you have placed my old friend, PUTNAM; you have not done him justice. I wish you would alter that part of your picture, and introduce a circumstance which actually happened, and which I can never forget. When the British troops advanced, the second time, to the attack of the redoubt, I, with the other officers, was in front of the line, to encourage the men; we had advanced very near the works, undisturbed, when an irregular fire, like a *feu-de-joie*, was poured in upon us; it was cruelly fatal. The troops fell back; and, when I looked to the right and left, I saw not one officer standing. I glanced my eye to the enemy, and saw several young men leveling their pieces at me; I knew their excellence as marksmen, and considered myself gone. At that moment my old friend, PUTNAM, rushed forward, and, striking up the muzzles of their pieces with his sword, cried out, 'For God's sake, my lads, don't fire at that man; I love him as I do my brother.' We were so near each other that I heard his words distinctly. He was obeyed; I bowed, thanked him, and walked away unmolested." Colonel JOHN TRUMBULL says of Colonel SMALL that "he had the character of an honorable, upright man, and could have no conceivable motive for deviating from the truth, in relating the circumstances to me. I therefore believe them true!" The above is also vouched for by Colonel DANIEL PUTNAM, who states that "his father related the same circumstance to him, soon after the battle; and that there was also an interview between Colonel SMALL and General PUTNAM, on the lines, between Prospect Hill and Bunker's Hill, not long after the action, solicited by the Colonel, for the purpose of renewing their old acquaintance, and of tendering his thanks to the General for preserving his life."

Colonel SWETT also, in speaking of this affair, in his work, page 39, says, that when the muskets were leveled at the Colonel, and PUTNAM appeared, "each recognized in the other an old friend and fellow-soldier; the tie was sacred: PUTNAM threw up the deadly muskets with his sword, and arrested his fate. He begged his men to spare that officer, as dear to him as a brother. The General's humane and chivalrous generosity excited in them new admiration, and his friend retired unhurt."

In regard to Major MONCRIEF, and his connections with PUTNAM, I find a relation of the whole affair in *Frothingham's* work, pages 111 and 112, as follows: "On the 6th of June, an exchange of prisoners took place. 'Dr. WARREN (*Essex Gazette of that date*) and Brigadier-General PUTNAM, in a phaeton,' together with other officers of the American army, and the prisoners, the whole escorted by the Wethersfield company, Captain CHESTER, entered the town of Charlestown, and marched to the ferry, when, upon a signal being given, Major MONCRIEF landed from the *Lively*, in order to receive the prisoners, and see his old friend, General PUTNAM. Their meeting was truly cordial and affectionate. The wounded privates were soon sent on board the *Lively*; but Major MONCRIEF and the other officers returned with General PUTNAM and Dr. WARREN to the house of Dr. FOSTER, where an entertainment was provided for them." At three o'clock, the exchange of prisoners took place; and, between five and six o'clock, Major MONCRIEF and General PUTNAM parted company, and returned to their respective camps. "The whole was conducted," (*says Frothingham*) "*with the utmost decency and good humor!*"

Thus are two instances of a renewal of old acquaintance, and the tendering of brotherly sympathy and courtesy in a "truly cordial and affectionate" manner, twisted by Mr. DAWSON into acts of treason; and General PUTNAM, the noble old hero, who, in the midst of hostilities and bloodshed, could not altogether forget the comrades of other days, and could not stifle all of his feelings of brotherly friendship, nor fail to pay it homage, even on the battle-field, must be branded with the charge of being a second traitor Arnold! It is thus that General Putnam's detractors have ever proceeded: turning his acts of courage into acts of cowardice; his sympathy and tenderness into evidences of treason; his great, and almost herculean, efforts and energies into sluggishness and lax energy; and his well-deserved fame into disgrace and ignominy!

In Mr. Dawson's letter, he makes reference to letters written, as he claims, by General Washington, wherein that General censures Putnam, and speaks disparagingly of him as a military officer. Of this I know not what to think. I cannot take oath that General Washington did not write such letters, nor can I bring myself to believe that he used deceit and prevarication in the premises. But it is withal an undeniable fact that there is a letter now in existence, in General Washington's own handwriting, dated January 30, 1776, in which he says, "*General Putnam is a valuable man, and a fine executive officer!*" And General Washington also wrote General Putnam a very affectionate letter, after the close of hostilities, and, therefore, at a time when Washington would have a correct opinion of Putnam, if ever, gathered from a full knowledge of his whole actions, throughout the war. This letter is dated June, 1783, and reads as follows: "Dear Sir— Your favor of the 20th of May, I received with much pleasure; for I can assure you that among the many *worthy and meritorious officers* with whom I have had the happiness to be connected in service through the course of this war, and from whose cheerful assistance in the various and trying vicissitudes of a complicated contest, the *name of a Putnam is not forgotten ; nor will it be, but with that stroke of time* which shall obliterate from my mind the remembrance of all those toils and fatigues through which we have struggled, for the preservation and establishment of the rights, liberties, and independence of our country!"

Such are the sentiments of General WASHINGTON at the close of the war—a time when, if ever, he should be perfectly conversant with *all* the actions of PUTNAM, and when he could draw a correct, unbiased opinion of him. We have also a letter from JOSEPH REED, WASHINGTON's private secretary at the time of the siege of Boston, in which he writes to WASHINGTON, under date March 15, 1776, in reference to the contemplated siege, and uses the following words: "I supposed OLD PUT was to command the detachment intended for Boston, on the 5th instant, as I do not know any officer but himself *who could have been depended on for so hazardous a service!*" This letter may be found in "REED's *Life*," vol. II., p. 172. Says FROTHINGHAM, "No higher military testimony than this can be adduced; for REED was a soldier, and as capable of judging as any person in the army!"

I might go on, and fill the columns of this paper, for days yet, with such evidences of General PUTNAM's great gallantry and courage, combined with rare abilities and military tact, and an ever-burning zeal and ardor for the cause of American liberty; but it may not be. I feel that I have already overstepped the usual bounds of newspaper communications, and must bring this article to a close. But I cannot, in conclusion, refrain from giving an extract from the columns of the *Connecticut Courant*, wherein (in an article published soon after the battle of Bunker's Hill, in 1775) is clearly shown the popular feeling in regard to General PUTNAM in those "days that tried men's souls." The extract reads as follows : " In this list of heroes, it is needless to expatiate on the character and bravery of Major-General PUTNAM, whose capacity to form and execute great designs is known through Europe, and whose undaunted courage and martial abilities strike terror through all the hosts of Midianites, and have raised him to an incredible height in the esteem and friendship of his American brethren ; it is sufficient to say, that he seems to be inspired by God Almighty with a military genius, and formed to work wonders in the sight of those uncircumcised Philistines, at Boston and Bunker's Hill, who attempt to ravage this country, and defy the armies of the living God ! "

I have given these facts—gleaned from many and reliable sources—to the public, that people may not fall into Mr. DAWSON's way of thinking, in regard to General PUTNAM's character and services, without hearing both sides of the subject. If sound evidence, drawn from pure and unquestionable sources, is the thing needed to set at rest, for ever, General PUTNAM's detractors, then surely my article has not been written in vain, and will find a ready response in the hearts of the people, who have ever loved to revere " the name of a PUTNAM ! " I sincerely hope Mr. DAWSON will relieve himself of that passion which he has shown in his writings, and which, to use the mildest expression, certainly savors strongly of prejudice—and that in defiance of all historical facts—and come over to the ranks of the "true defenders of the faith." I am certain he will feel better himself—feel as if the hands of the people, the hearts of the people, the "*vox populi*," were with him, and not against him, in his labors as a historian.

   I am, sincerely,
     Your humble servant,
       "SELAH."

H. B. DAWSON'S THIRD LETTER.

[FROM THE "HARTFORD DAILY POST," AUGUST 2, 3, 4, 5, 6, 8, 9, 10, 11, AND 12, 1859.*]

WHITE PLAINS, N. Y., May 19, 1859.

To the Editor of the Hartford Daily Post:

MR. EDITOR : Your kind intentions, in attempting to furnish me with a copy of "*Selah's*" last letter, having been frustrated by some sympathizing friend and follower of General PUTNAM, I have been unable, until last night, to find even a portion of that extended production which appeared between April 20th and April 25th, and, in consequence of that mishap, I have been compelled to defer making any answer to it until this late date.

With your permission, Mr. Editor, I propose to notice some of the peculiarities of this elaborate performance—running through six numbers of the *Daily Post*—not with any hopes of convincing "*Selah*," or his coadjutor, who have produced it, of their error; but for the purpose of showing, to "the mass of the people of Connecticut," who

---

* DAWSON *vs.* SELAH.—We shall to-morrow commence the publication of HENRY B. DAWSON's reply to "*Selah*," relative to the life and services of General PUTNAM. Owing to its length, we have been obliged to delay its appearance, from time to time, to make room for other, and to us, more interesting matter. In justice to Mr. DAWSON, we would state, that his reply has been awaiting publication ever since the first of May. Some important matter has been added to it of subsequent date, however.—*Hartford Daily Post, August 1st,* 1859.

they are who have impudently assumed to themselves the honor of vindicating "the honor of Connecticut;" and of exposing, before an outraged people, the manner in which they have discharged that self-imposed, but important duty.

Before proceeding to that duty, however, I may be permitted to congratulate Connecticut on the good sense which "*Selah*" has displayed, FIRST, in surrendering, without a struggle, as he had previously done in respect to PUTNAM's birth-place, and other fictions, six out of seven of the positions he had taken in his second letter; and, SECONDLY, in securing the assistance of so able and so nimble an auxiliary as he whose handiwork, in such marked contrast to his own, is so apparent in the extended letter which is now before me. With such a "CHAMPION" as this, in the person of *the squire*, added to the profound skill, the high-toned honor, the chivalrous bearing, and the untiring love of enterprise which mark the character of *the knight*, "the honor of Connecticut," one would suppose, must now, if ever, be perfectly secure; and the good name of PUTNAM, in such a Don Quixote and Sancho Panza, must, at last, have found an appropriate, if not an irresistible protection.

In that portion of the letter which has been contributed by my old friend, "*Selah*," I find, for a wonder, nothing which is new. He has evidently desired to fall back on the laurels which he had previously gained; and, as a veteran of two campaigns, and in humble imitation of his great exemplar, PUTNAM, he now leaves to his subordinate the labor of fighting the battle, while he holds himself in readiness either to join in the retreat or to claim the honors, as circumstances may warrant.

As I have said already, I find, in the first part of the letter, nothing which is new. The same strain of personal abuse ; the same malignant perversion of language and of facts ; the same deliberate falsification of the record ; the same sneaking inuendoes, which, from the beginning, have marked " *Selah's* " course, are conspicuous in the beginning of this letter, and tell at once the story of its origin and the character of its author. It betrays the workmanship of him who manufactured " town records " and " opinions of the oldest inhabitants " to prove that PUTNAM was born in Pomfret, Connecticut ; of him who, from a reference to the gallantry of KNOWLTON's command in the action near Bunker's Hill, forged a charge that I had asserted they " skulked behind rail-fences," to dodge the bullets ; of him who paraded the authorities which I had cited on one subject, as my witnesses on other subjects in which I had never examined them. With that peculiar kind of assurance which none but the most unprincipled ever display in public, he attempts, also, by inuendo, to invalidate the authorities by which I have met and exposed his falsehoods—sneering at what he pleases to term my " budget of private letters," " written, perhaps, by some one, and, perhaps, at some time, now to be found, perhaps, somewhere." I need only say, in answer to this elegant sentence, that I have cited no " *private* letters ;" that the names of the writers of nearly all of them, the dates when, and the places where they were written, were all cited in full--the space which would have been necessary to print the entire documents forbidding any more extended reference to them. As " *Selah's* " faithful squire can tell him, if that is necessary, they have all been published, in such a form that no court in Connecticut can, legally, exclude them, should they be offered in evidence; besides which, as an additional proof of "*Selah's*" duplicity, I have the most indisputable evidence that authentic copies of these identical letters were before him while he was writing this very communication.

In unison with this, also, is the blustering offer of ten dollars, which "*Selah*" makes, in behalf of the Secretary of State, for "a duly authenticated copy of the letter of Governor TRUMBULL, of Connecticut, to the BARON VAN DER CAPELLAN, in which the former informs the latter that General PUTNAM did not command at Bunker's Hill;" and the assurance that "the money will be forthcoming." I have not referred to any such letter; and if I had done so, the assurance of "*Selah*" that ten dollars would be given for "a duly authenticated copy," would furnish but a poor guarantee that his draft would be honored. I cited a letter from Governor JONATHAN TRUMBULL, dated "*Lebanon, August* 31, 1779," and addressed to "BARON J. D. VAN DER CAPELLAN, *Seigneur du Pol, Membre des Nobles de la Province d'Overysul*, &c.," in answer to a letter which the Baron had addressed to him from "*Zwol, 7th December*, 1778," in which the Governor uses these words:

"On the 16th June, 1775, it was resolved to form a post on that part of the high grounds of Charlestown nighest to the town of Boston; from which we should have the power of annoying the enemy, both in the town and harbor. The plan for the execution of this determination *was not well formed:* and the executive part, dependent on officers and troops unacquainted with discipline, *was still more inattentively prosecuted*. About six hundred men, with arms and entrenching tools, were marched down in the evening, and broke ground at twelve o'clock. The entrenchments, for want of engineers, were in a similar style with the preparatory steps, *sufficiently injudicious*. At daybreak, of the 17th of June, we were discovered by the enemy, and a cannonade immediately commenced, which continued, with little interruption, though as little execution, till afternoon. Meantime the unfortunate six hundred, fatigued with labor and want of sleep, and quite inadequate in number to the defense of the post they had been employed to form, were not only *not* relieved by fresh men, but *not* even furnished with provisions and liquors for their refreshment, or the extraordinary ammunition which they must necessarily expend. In this situation they were attacked, at three o'clock P.M., by twelve hundred British troops, under the command of General HOWE. Yet even when thus *unsupported by their brethren*, exposed to the fire of several ships of war and batteries, and the attack of double their number of men, they maintained their post with determined firmness, and repeatedly forced the enemy to give way; till General HOWE, being strongly reinforced, *and finding themselves still abandoned to their fate*, their ammunition exhausted, THEIR COMMANDING OFFICER, THE BRAVE GENERAL WARREN, and near half their number killed or wounded, the remaining few fled, and left the enemy masters of the field. To add to the horrors of this *new* scene, the town of Charlestown was set on fire, and reduced to ashes. Perhaps there have been few more obstinate battles ever fought: near one half the troops engaged, on each side, being either killed or wounded; that is, of the British, eleven hundred, and of the Americans more than three hundred."

I have cited all that Governor TRUMBULL said on this subject, in order to show what the people of Connecticut thought on the subject in 1779; and " *Selah* " and the Secretary of State are welcome to all they can make out of it for the glorification of General PUTNAM. I beg to remind the Honorable Secretary, at the same time, that *the originals* of both the Baron's letter and the Governor's answer are in the Library of the Massachusetts Historical Society; that *my* copy of the document, formerly owned by the DWIGHTS of Connecticut, and " DULY *authenticated*," cost me seventy-five cents; that the same opportunity still exists to obtain copies; and that nine dollars, or thereabouts, may be saved from the reward which he offered, and may be invested in Charter Oak charms, for the consolation of " *Selah*." When Governor TRUMBULL wrote this letter, and for many years afterwards, it was not pretended that PUTNAM commanded in "the Battle of Bunker's Hill," nor had his name been used, in any manner, as a prominent actor in that engagement; and the writer was no more called on to say that PUTNAM did *not* command at Bunker's Hill, than I am to say that " *Selah*" is a gentleman and a scholar, or to mention any other fact or fiction which is foreign to the subject. It is a very significant fact, however, that while the Governor condemns the management of the affair, and the failure to strengthen the forces and to supply them with ammunition, he never mentions General PUTNAM's name, but, on the contrary, calls " the brave General WARREN" "their commanding officer."

Passing thence to " *Selah's*" next subject—that " in referring to the exploits of PUTNAM in the wolf-den, at Horseneck, and the French War," I have " adduced nothing to refute them that has a semblance of validity or argument." I do not feel called upon to enlarge on those subjects. A discriminating public has already decided between " *Selah*" and myself, in the evidence which each has adduced; and my opponent, in spite of his inclinations to the contrary, has prudently bowed to its verdict, without appeal, and discontinued the discussion. On one subject, however—*that of Bunker's Hill*—he has received a fresh supply of ammunition and a reinforcement, in which respect he has fared better than the gallant troops of whom he pretends to speak ; and, taking courage from that circumstance, he proposes to make that subject "a test ;" and, from " the evidence" which *he* adduces "in reference to General PUTNAM's position in that battle, to build up, at once, a monument of that hero's glory and Mr. DAWSON's shame." I confess I did not, before, suppose I possessed so much consequence as to secure so handsome a compliment. ISRAEL PUTNAM and HENRY B. DAWSON receiving, at the same time, from the same hands, the honor of an undivided "*monument!*" It is true that to *him* it is to be a monument of "*glory*," while to *me* it is to be one of "*shame ;*" yet it is to be "*a monument :*" and when it is remembered that epitaphs generally speak falsely, and that both sides of a subject are seldom looked at, now-a-days, by the same persons, it matters but little what is on the other side, and an eulogy of PUTNAM might as well appear there as any other inscription. Would it not be well, in this connection, for "*Selah*" to take counsel of the past, and to recollect the monument of "shame" which HAMAN erected for MORDECAI; and, having done so, to inquire to what use that "monument" was actually put, and to take warning ?

I have now come to the second part of the communication, signed "*Selah*"—that in which the ingenuity of his faithful squire has been so elaborately employed. We may readily know a man from the company he keeps ; and this assistant "CHAMPION" of PUTNAM's character differs but little, except in scholarship, from his veteran chief. If I do not mistake, he also is a soldier of fortune, and ready to cast his services in support of that cause which pays the best—alternately "flaunting '*Sustinet qui transtulet*'" in the eyes of Governor TRYON, in behalf of the injured WOOSTER: and filling the columns of the *Hartford Courant* with eulogistic essays on the greatness and goodness of PUTNAM, while the communication now under consideration shows that, like "*Selah*," he does not hesitate to manufacture testimony to support his cause, when he fails to find it ready for his use.

He opens his part by asserting that "it is a well-known fact that PUTNAM held a regularly commissioned command of the Continental troops previous to the battle of Bunker Hill"—a falsehood, to begin with, which any school-boy of your common schools can refute. It is true that during the session in April, 1775, (*April* 26,) the Assembly of Connecticut, "finding it prudent and necessary to make open preparation, passed 'An act for Assembling, Equipping, &c., a number of the Inhabitants of the Colony, for the special defense and safety thereof;'" and it is equally true that ISRAEL PUTNAM was appointed Captain of the First Company of the Third Regiment, Colonel of that Regiment, and Second Brigadier-General—Generals WOOSTER and SPENCER being his superiors in office; but that appointment did not give him "a regularly commissioned command of the Continental troops," or any other command beyond those to which I have referred—the Connecticut troops, who had been raised "for the special defense and safety of that colony." If Mr. DAY's official certificate shows anything more than this, it shows a falsehood; for where did the Assembly of Connecticut, from which he received all the power he possessed, receive any authority to legislate for the government of any person beyond the limits of that colony? and how could the commission, which the government of that colony had issued, authorize him to command the Continental troops, which had never been heard of when he received that commission? In fact, he was, like the officers whom Connecticut commissions at the present day, an officer of the Connecticut troops, while they are on duty in Connecticut, or under her authority, and nothing more. In due course of time portions of these troops and their officers, by order of the General Assembly, at its April session, went "to the relief of the people at the Bay," and PUTNAM went with them. His commission, however, was as so much white paper the moment he crossed the line which separated Connecticut from Rhode Island, except among the Connecticut troops, by whom alone his authority was recognized; and not a shadow of authority did he possess or exercise over the troops of any other colony. The extent of the authority which these officers exercised, even among their own people, while outside of Connecticut, is evident from the fact that, after a few days' experience, "a large portion of these minute men," who had proceeded to Massachusetts from Connecticut, "soon returned to their homes." (*Frothingham's Siege of Boston*, p. 100.) On the other hand, "although the orders of the day were copied by all the troops, and a voluntary obedience, it is stated, was yielded to General WARD by the whole army, as the commander-in-chief;" (*Frothingham*, p. 101,) that obedience was not general, and difficulties ensued. In fact, at the time of the action on Bunker's Hill, the only troops which General

WARD had any authority to command were those of Massachusetts and New Hampshire—Connecticut, through its Committee of War, retaining the command of her's until June 19, (*Minutes of the Committee of War*, Monday, June 19, 1775, A.M.,) and Rhode Island that of her "army of observation," until June 28, (*Minutes of the General Assembly*, June 28, 1775,) and this accounts for the fact that the only troops who could be sent by General WARD, to strengthen the detachment on Bunker Hill, were the New Hampshire troops, under Colonels STARK and REED.* Such was the standing of ISRAEL PUTNAM on the 17th June, 1775, when "the battle of Bunker Hill" was fought—a

---

* The following extract from an interesting letter, written by Hon. JOHN ADAMS, many years after the battle, will show the well-settled opinion of that great man on the subject now under consideration :

QUINCY, JUNE 19, 1818.

DEAR SIR : I have received your letter of the 16th. My letter to Colonel DANIEL PUTNAM, of the 5th, is at his and your disposal. You may publish any part of it, or the whole, at your discretion.

I wish the young gentlemen of the age would undertake an analytical investigation of the constitution of the army at Cambridge, and of the detachment from it at Bunker's Hill and Breed's Hill, on the 16th and 17th of June.

The army at Cambridge *was not a national army*, for there was no nation. *It was not a United States army*, for there were no united colonies ; for, if it could be said in any sense that the colonies were united, the centre of their union—the Congress at Philadelphia—had not adopted or acknowledged the army at Cambridge. *It was not a New England army* ; for New England had not associated. New England had no legal legislature, nor any common executive authority, even upon the principles of original authority, or even of original power in the people.

Massachusetts had *her* army, Connecticut *her* army, New Hampshire *her* army, and Rhode Island *her* army. These *four* armies met at Cambridge, and imprisoned the British army in Boston. But who was the sovereign of this united, *or rather*, CONGREGATED *army*, and who its commander-in-chief? IT HAD NONE. PUTNAM, POOR and GREENE, were as independent of WARD as WARD was of them. None of them but WARD was subject to the orders of the Massachusetts Provincial Congress. I desire to know from whom PUTNAM received his commission, and from whom POOR received his commission ; and I pray let the commissions of WARD, PUTNAM, POOR and GREENE be all produced. * * * * * But, sir, I must suppress a thousand questions, and conclude.

Your humble servant,

GEORGE BRINLEY, ESQ.   JOHN ADAMS.

Colonial General, exercising no legal authority, except over the Connecticut troops; and, with them, recognizing the right of no man or body of men outside of the Connecticut Committee of War, to issue orders for their government. On the 19th of June—two days after the action, and the same day on which the Committee of War had ordered him to yield obedience to General WARD— he was appointed a Major-General in the Continental service; and it was not until General WASHINGTON had reached Cambridge that he received his commission. *With these facts before him at the time when he penned the paragraph in question, as was the case,* what can be said in favor of one who could *deliberately falsify the record* to support his favorite theory? This is shown from the fact that "*Selah*" cites, in another part of this letter, from the very work which contains the printed records referred to. I repeat, therefore, that General PUTNAM was not a Continental officer previous to, or at the time of the battle of Bunker Hill; that he recognized the authority of no one but the Committee of War in Connecticut, to issue any orders for the government of the troops of that colony; and that he possessed no authority (and could enforce none) over the troops of either of the other colonies.

The next subject which is introduced is a statement that Governor TRUMBULL ordered PUTNAM to "repair at once to Cambridge, and take charge of the troops, and he would make out his commission, and send it on after him;" that "thus we have abundant evidence that PUTNAM was the commander-in-chief of the American troops before the battle;" and that, "taking this for granted, it is but fair to suppose that he also commanded them in the battle." In the perusal of this paragraph, I have been at a loss whether to attribute it to the ignorance or to the dishonesty of the writer. As I have shown already, PUTNAM was an officer of the colony of Connecticut, commanding the Third Regiment of Connecticut troops, and subject only to the orders of the General Assembly, or the Committee of War in that colony. He had marched to Boston, by order of the Governor, in conformity with law; and as the superior officer, had also orders "to take charge of the troops there." But is any one so void of common sense as to suppose that Governor TRUMBULL issued such an order, with the expectation or desire that the New Hampshire, Massachusetts, and Rhode Island troops would recognize PUTNAM as their commander-in-chief; or even that PUTNAM so understood it? At the period in question, Massachusetts had eleven thousand five hundred men in the field, under the veteran WARD; New Hampshire, one thousand two hundred, under the same officer; Connecticut, two thousand three hundred, thus placed under PUTNAM, in the absence of his superiors; and Rhode Island, one thousand, under General GREENE, (*Frothingham*, 101,) and he must be ambitious of honor who would assume, as this writer has done, that Massachusetts, Rhode Island and New Hampshire would so tamely submit to the dictation of Connecticut, or yield the command of their troops to an officer of her appointment, who had not even received his commission from the hands of her Governor.

Next comes a melo-dramatic account of a supposed council, wherein General WARD, Doctor WARREN and General PUTNAM are represented as discussing "the subject of fortifying Bunker's Hill," with all "the effect" which excites, to so great a degree, the admiration of the pit in the old Bowery. In answer to this silly interlude, it is only necessary to say that this measure was adopted in the Committee of Safety of Massachusetts, of which neither WARD nor PUTNAM were members. A fac-simile copy of the original order, signed by "BENJA. WHITE, *Chairman*," may be found in FROTHINGHAM's *Siege of Boston*, page 116, and the entire proceedings, at length, appear in the *Minutes of the Committee of Safety*, June 15, 1775. I might also refer to the impossibility of PUTNAM conducting such a conversation as is here described; and in evidence of his accomplishments, I refer to the following *correct* copy of an order which he issued while commanding in the city of Philadelphia in 1776:

head quartors, ye 14 of December, 1776.

All ofisors and solders boath Thoas that are Newly inlisted into the contenontol sarwis Thos of the flieing Camp the melishey and all the Inhabitence of this City are requested to parad to morrow morning at 9 o'clock at the Markit to go on fitig to fortify this city and so on Every morning tel farther orders.   ISRAEL PUTNAM.

Before proceeding to an examination of the main question, on its own merits, allow me to inquire what testimony has been adduced by my opponents to prove that General PUTNAM was present, either in the redoubt or behind the rail-fence, during the action of June 17, 1775.

First. We have the jottings down of floating rumors, by President STILES, of Yale College, all of which were disproved by his subsequent entry, on the 23d June, which was made on General PUTNAM's own authority.

Second. We have a *false* quotation from Judge GROSVENOR's letter to DANIEL PUTNAM—"'he was in a Connecticut regiment,' who, with a much larger number of Massachusetts troops, under Colonel PRESCOTT, were ordered by General Putnam to march on the evening, &c." The original, which is now before me,* reads thus : "Being under the command of General Putnam, part of our regiment, and a much larger number of Massachusetts troops, under Colonel Prescott, were ordered to march on the evening, &c." Any school-boy can see that, while in the original letter the authority of General Putnam and that of Colonel Prescott were equal, each commanding his own party only, the interpolation of "by General Putnam," *at the close of the paragraph,* by "*Selah,*" makes a cool, deliberate falsehood, and brands the author of the fraud with all the shame which attaches to him who feloniously removes his neighbor's land-mark.

Third. We have an extract from Mr. Whitney's funeral sermon—the very first claim which was ever made in behalf of General Putnam. As General Putnam never claimed any such honor while he lived, even when he was relating his services as a basis for a claim on his country—his acknowledged occupation of Prospect Hill having satisfied him, even in that emergency—I do not feel called upon further to show the worthlessness of this authority.

Fourth. The extract from Major Jackson's diary is such that I do not object to it as authority, inasmuch as it does not disprove any statement which I have made.

Fifth. We have a reference to John Boyle's diary, which, "*Selah*" says, "was kept *at that time.*" While the statements extracted therefrom do not disprove anything I have said, why does "*Selah*" unnecessarily tell a falsehood in connection with the book? If he knows enough about this diary to quote from it, he knows it was *not*

---

* The letter here referred to can be found by the reader, if he desires to continue the investigation, in the *Portfolio,* fifth series, vol. 6, pages 9–11.

"kept at that time," nor for many months afterwards; and even then, that it was mostly a compilation from the newspapers of the day, and in the language of these useful but rather uncertain publications. By this special clause did "*Selah*" propose to repeat the same fraud on the public which he attempted in the case of Judge GROSVENOR's letter, already referred to, or was it done for *my* especial benefit, in the present discussion?

Sixth. RIVINGTON's "*New York Gazette*" may serve a very good purpose when it is sustained by more reliable authorities; yet I very much question if it proves anything in opposition to the testimony of those who were eye-witnesses of the circumstances in question, unless, it may be, the very great necessity under which "*Selah*" labors for a little evidence to sustain his errors. Those who know the character of RIVINGTON's *Gazette*, in all which relates to the *popular* cause, need not be told that it cannot be relied on—the *Royal Printer*, in New York, having been poor authority on all *popular* movements which transpired in Boston.

Seventh. "Colonel SWETT" is cited and lauded as a very paragon of authenticity. My opinions of this gentleman's works on PUTNAM are already before your readers; and, with the fact before me, that it was he who besmeared a historical fact with the filth and slime of partisan malignity, I do not hesitate to say that I cannot discriminate between his word, on this subject, and the documents which he has mutilated for party purposes, and all are alike discarded as unworthy of confidence.

Eighth. We have allusions to "affidavits of Governor BROOKS, Colonel WADE, Judge GROSVENOR, Major LYMAN,

Colonel Webb, Anderson Miner, Joshua Yeomans, Simeon Noyes, and many others," to prove the exploits of Putnam in covering the retreat of the Americans. I beg leave to say that Judge Grosvenor makes no allusion to Putnam in this connection, his words being, "which our brave Captain Knowlton perceiving, ordered a retreat of his men, in which he was sustained by two companies under the command of Captains Clark and Chester." Yeomans makes no allusion to the retreat. Noyes says, "When we were retreating, he rode up to us with his tent and tent-poles on his horse, and asked "why we were retreating?" Colonel Wade speaks of the retreat, without referring to any very remarkable conduct on the part of Putnam.

Ninth. We have the hearsay testimony of Colonel Wade, Ethan Clark, William Williams, and the publisher of an anonymous portrait—none of whom possessed any peculiar advantages for acquiring information over their neighbors in Providence, Lebanon, or London, and all of whom have been contradicted by those who were engaged in the action, as well as by the records of the transactions, connected therewith, to which their testimony relates.

Tenth. Dr. James Thacher is cited to prove that Putnam commanded at Bunker's Hill—"on the American side, Generals Putnam, Warren, Pomeroy, and Colonel Prescott, were emphatically the heroes of the day, and their unparalleled efforts were crowned with glory!" In this extract, "*Selah*" says, "It will be seen that Thacher places Putnam first, thus seeming to give him precedence also in command." I have before me a copy of "*The Military Journal*"—the work from which the above is taken—and find "*Selah*," or his squire, has imitated their leader in this controversy, by *mutilating the text*, in order to sustain a falsehood. THACHER says (page 26), "It was deemed important that our troops should possess themselves of this eminence (*Bunker's Hill*) before the enemy could occupy it. Accordingly orders were given *to Colonel* PRESCOTT, a veteran of the last war, with one thousand men, to march silently in the evening of the 16th June," &c. Again, on the same page, without assigning the command to either of them, he says, "Generals PUTNAM, WARREN and POMEROY animated and encouraged the troops with their presence." But, on page 29, appear the words, with little variation, as cited by "*Selah*," followed, however, by these important remarks, which *he has suppressed*, in order to make Dr. THACHER support what he has expressly denied—"The incomparable Colonel PRESCOTT marched at the head of the detachment, and though several general officers were present, *he retained the command during the action.* He displayed a native, daring bravery altogether unrivaled, and infused the conquering spirit of a soldier into the hearts of all who were under his command, and crowned himself with immortal honor." Such, Mr. Editor, is the manner in which my opponents are conducting this investigation; and in this manner have your readers been imposed on by these self-constituted guardians of "the honor of Connecticut."

Eleventh. "*Selah*" next favors us with extracts from the letter of a nameless officer of the British army, in Boston, to his friend in England, which he coolly says, "all go to establish PUTNAM's claims to the honor, not only of commandership, but of having taken a brave and daring part in the strife." Your readers need but see the words of the officer to be convinced of the deception which my opponents have employed. "After the skirmish of the 17th, we even commended the troops of PUTNAM, who fought so gallantly, *pro aris et focis.*" PUTNAM's troops did "fight gallantly, *pro aris et focis,*" but KNOWLTON led them, while PUTNAM, as we shall presently show, was not present—the paragraph in question making no allusion whatever in support of PUTNAM's "commandership," or PUTNAM's "presence in the strife." Again, the officer, speaking of the secrecy with which the expedition was conducted, says, "Generals CLINTON and BURGOYNE knew not of it till the morning, though the town did in general, and PUTNAM in particular." I confess I do not see wherein this sentence, over which "*Selah*" manifests so much pleasure, has any bearing on the questions at issue; or wherein it proves or disproves anything which either "*Selah*" or I have asserted. As General PUTNAM gave the orders to the Connecticut troops, on the evening of the 16th, and as he accompanied them on their "secret" and silent march—leaving them at work on the hill at one o'clock—I can see no reason why he should "not have known of it," in particular, nor have I ever supposed or argued differently. I have no desire to limit the pleasure either of "*Selah*" or his squire, however; and if they find comfort in these extracts, let them enjoy the feast.

Twelfth. "*Selah*" refers to sundry *ex parte* affidavits which Colonel SWETT and his associates, under the direction and at the expense of the Federalists of Boston, prepared and caused to be executed and verified, in or about 1818, for the purpose of securing the defeat of the Democratic candidate for Governor of Massachusetts, Major-General HENRY DEARBORN, who had fearlessly exposed the true character of General PUTNAM a short time before.

Colonel SWETT " devoted two months of his life, night and day, to this subject," (*Letter of Colonel Swett to Ballard & Wright,* 1819,) to say nothing of like services by other party hacks, who were equally zealous and not less unscrupulous; and when the principles, or rather the want of principles, which actuate all such gentlemen, when thus employed, are considered, the peculiar character of these papers—especially that of those of them which were executed by men who could neither read writing or sign their own names—will be readily appreciated. In another part of this letter I shall examine the contents of these affidavits; and if your readers will refer to that division of my subject, they will see that "*Selah*" has added to the interest which attaches to these affidavits *per se,* when *he* or his squire, says, " they all agree that PUTNAM was on Bunker's and Breed's Hills, both in the night of the 16th, and during the day of the 17th of June, 1775. They all agree, too, that he there performed the duties devolving upon a commander ; and that they, as well as their comrades in arms, always considered him their commander on that day."

Thirteenth. We have Mr. FROTHINGHAM's "*Siege of Boston*" produced as evidence to show that Major MONCRIEFFE and General PUTNAM were intimate friends in 1775; and that at that time they met, in the exchange of prisoners, and parted " with the utmost decency and good humor." From this "*Selah*" affects to prove that I have " twisted " an incident which occurred before Boston, in 1775, into " an act of treason" in the city of New York, in 1776. I beg my opponents will not thus abandon their favorite. It was the fact of Major MONCRIEFFE's acquaintance with PUTNAM, and his knowledge of the General's weakness, which led that distinguished officer to dispatch his own daughter as a spy into New York, and to intrust her within the General's family. No father would thus have hazarded the life of a talented daughter, had he not felt assured, beforehand, that she would be safe; and in no hands could he have more properly placed her, than in those of a personal friend, whose patriotism was deposited in his pocket-book; and whose interest, in the cause of the United States, fluctuated with his pecuniary interests.

Lastly. We have extracts of letters from General WASHINGTON and JOSEPH REED, and of an editorial in "*The Connecticut Courant*," which "*Selah*," like a dealer in quack medicines, parades as certificates of the wonderful character of his article. It will become my duty, before closing this letter, to invite the attention of your readers to the opinions of these same officers, and others, respecting PUTNAM, as shown by their acts, during the dark days of our country's history. Until that time I shall let these extracts pass unnoticed.

We come now to the first grand division of my opponents' labors—the occupation of the heights in the night of June 16, 1775—in the examination of which I propose to be as brief as possible, consistent with my desire that "*Selah*" and his assistant may have no just excuse for misrepresenting me, or of misunderstanding my meaning.

I. WHY, AND BY WHOM, WAS THE OCCUPATION OF THE HEIGHTS NEAR CHARLESTOWN ORIGINALLY ORDERED? My friends in Hartford say it "was to draw the enemy out of Boston, on ground where they might be met on equal terms;" and, on that hypothesis, they build up the bombastic conversation which, as they assert, took place "in the American camp," between Generals WARD and PUTNAM and Doctor WARREN, to which allusion has heretofore been made. In assigning this as the reason, however, my opponents have been only the faint imitators of their leader, Colonel SWETT, in his "*History of the Bunker Hill Battle, A.D.* 1827," page 14, forgetting, as he forgot, that "the American camp" was not the origin of the subject; that Doctor WARREN had no voice in "the Council of War," and could not, therefore, have taken part in its discussions; and that as Generals WARD and PUTNAM held no seats in "the Committee of Safety," where it did originate, they could not have taken part in the discussion of the subject before that body—where alone, if anywhere, Doctor WARREN could have taken the part which has been assigned to him.

As the records, previously cited, show that my opponents have mistaken the character of the body from whence the project of the occupation of the heights proceeded, so they have also erred in their theory respecting the purpose of that movement. Instead of desiring thereby "to draw the enemy out of Boston," as my opponents maintain, the records show that the very reverse of this was the object. The resolutions of the Committee of Safety—the original authority in the premises—open with this preamble, "*In Committee of Safety, Cambridge, June* 15, 1775. Whereas, it appears of Importance to the Safety of this Colony that possession of the Hill, Called Bunker's hill in Charlestown be Securely kept and defended; and allso some one hill or hills on Dorchester neck be likewise Secured. Therefore, Resolved Unanimously," &c. On the 7th July, 1775, the Provincial Congress of Massachusetts ordered the Committee of Safety to "draw up and transmit to Great Britain a fair and impartial account of the late battle at Charlestown, as soon as possible;" and, on the

25th of the same month, that committee made its report, which commences with these words: "In obedience to the above order of Congress, this committee have inquired into the premises, and, upon the best information obtained, find that the commanders of the New England army had, about the 14th ult., received advice that General GAGE had issued orders for a party of the troops under his command to post themselves on Bunker's Hill, a promontory just at the entrance of the peninsula of Charlestown, which orders were soon to be executed. Upon which it was determined, with the advice of this Committee, to send a party, who might erect some fortifications upon said hill, and defeat this design of our enemies;" and, lastly, an entry in the diary of Rev. Dr. BELKNAP, Oct. 20, 1775, on information received from General WARD's aid, confirms this statement;[*] from all of which it is evident that the object of the movement was to confine the enemy within the town, rather than "to draw him out;" that the Committee of Safety, instead of "the American camp," was the scene of the original movement in the premises; and that the part said to have been taken by Generals WARD and PUTNAM, from the fact that these officers could not have been present in the committee, is simply ridiculous.

II. FROM WHOM DID THE ORDERS FINALLY PROCEED, AND

---

[*] "After dining with General WARD, I returned to Cambridge; in the evening, visited and conversed with General PUTNAM. WARD appears to be a calm, cool, thoughtful man; PUTNAM, a rough, fiery genius.

"In conversation with Mr. WARD at Roxbury, I learned that the reason of our throwing up the intrenchment at Charlestown, on the night of the 16th June, was, that there had been intelligence received, such as could be depended on, that the regulars had determined to make a push for Cambridge, after the arrival of their three generals and reinforcements, who landed a few days before."—*Dr. Belknap's Diary, Oct. 20th, 1775.*

The "Mr. WARD" referred to was "Mr. JOSHUA WARD, aid-de-camp to the General," as will be seen by reference to the Doctor's diary, "*Oct. 19th.*"

TO WHOM WERE THEY DIRECTED? It will be recollected that my opponents stated, (*Daily Post*, Monday, April 18,) "we have abundant evidence that General PUTNAM was the commander-in-chief of the American troops before the battle;" and if this is true, the source from whence the orders proceeded is no longer in doubt. In that case the orders must have proceeded from General PUTNAM, and no other officer could have assumed the authority; yet the facts, as shown by the documents, do not sustain that theory. The troops to whom the orders were issued were WILLIAM PRESCOTT'S, FRYE'S and BRIDGE'S regiments of Massachusetts troops, and part of PUTNAM'S regiment of Connecticut troops (FROTHINGHAM'S *Siege of Boston*, p. 121; *Colnecol William Prescott's letter to Hon. John Adams*, Aug. 25, 1775; *Capt. Joseph Chester to Rev. Joseph Fish*, July 22, 1775.) The order books of the "Massachusetts army," on this subject, read thus: "JUNE 16. FRYE'S, BRIDGE'S, and WM. PRESCOTT'S regiments to parade this evening at 6 o'clock, with all the entrenching tools in this encampment." It will be seen from this order—copied from Captain FENNO'S order-book—that General WARD made no pretensions to the command of the Connecticut troops, the reason for which I have already alluded to, while the orders to the latter were issued by their senior commanding officer present, General PUTNAM. This is shown from the letter of Judge GROSVENOR, a Lieutenant in PUTNAM'S company, and, it is said, his son-in-law, addressed on the 30th April, 1818, to PUTNAM'S son, Colonel DANIEL PUTNAM. This letter, which has been mutilated and incorrectly copied by Colonel SWETT and some of his auxiliaries, opens with these words: "Being under the Command of General PUTNAM, part of our regiment, and a larger number of Massachusetts troops, under Colonel PRESCOTT, were ordered to march," &c. Thus were the detachments from the two "armies" ordered to the work of fortifying the hill—those belonging to the Massachusetts army by their commander, General WARD, and those belonging to the Connecticut forces by General PUTNAM; and the pretensions of my opponents that PUTNAM was the commander-in-chief of the entire force then before Boston, are put at rest.

III. DID PUTNAM ACCOMPANY THE EXPEDITION, AND IF SO, IN WHAT CAPACITY? The testimony of several who were present throw sufficient light on the subject, and the apparent contradiction of the witnesses—more apparent than real—is less important than some have supposed. In this connection, however, it is proper to premise, that in no part of "*Selah's*" correspondence is there a more total disregard of the requirements of truth than in his comments on the depositions of the soldiers who fought on Breed's Hill. In that portion of the letter which appeared in the *Post* of Thursday, April 21, "*Selah's*" assistant says, "in their depositions they all agree that PUTNAM was on Bunker's and Breed's Hill, both on the night of the 16th and during the day of the 17th of June, 1775. They all agree, too," he continues, "that he there performed the duties devolving upon a commander; and that they, as well as their comrades in arms, always considered him their commander on that day." In this place I have to examine only that portion of "all" these depositions which relates to the part which PUTNAM took in the expedition now under consideration, leaving that portion which relates to the action of the 17th June for another time.

The testimony which "*Selah*" has adduced, although adroitly mixed up by his assistant, in order to conceal the true character of the greater part of it, is composed of three distinct elements: *First*, that of Connecticut troops who were in the expedition; *Second*, that of Massachusetts troops, who were also in the expedition; and, *Third*, that of persons who were not present, and could know nothing about the matter, except from the information of others.

Commencing with the last class—the alleged testimony of those who were not present—we find the depositions of REUBEN KEMP, RICHARD GILCHRIST, EBENEZER BEAN and SAMUEL BASSETT, of Colonel STARK's New Hampshire troops; JOHN BARKER, BENJ. MANN and ENOS LAKE, of Colonel REED's New Hampshire troops; ISAAC BASSETT, ABIEL BUGBEE, JAMES CLARK, Colonel DANIEL PUTNAM and JOSIAH HILL, of General PUTNAM's Connecticut regiment; Major JOHN BURNHAM, SIMEON NOYES, Captain WADE, Lieutenant JOSEPH WHITMORE and PHILIP JOHNSON, of Colonel LITTLE's Massachusetts regiment; JOS. TRASK, Deacon MILLAR, ENOCH BALDWIN, JOHN HOPKINS, Mr. THOMPSON and WILLIAM DICKSON, of Colonel GARDNER's Massachusetts regiment; Sergeant JOB SPAFFORD, of WARD's Massachusetts regiment; A. DICKERSON, of Colonel WOODBRIDGE's Massachusetts regiment; BENJAMIN BULLARD, of Colonel BREWER's Massachusetts regiment; JOHN HOLDEN and SAMUEL JONES, of Colonel DOOLITTLE's Massachusetts regiment; WM. MARDEN, of Colonel GERRISH's Massachusetts regiment; GEO. LEACH, of Colonel WHITCOMB's Massachusetts regiment; DANIEL JACKSON and FRANCIS GREEN, of FOSTER's Massachusetts artillery; Major ELIHU LYMAN, ANDERSON MINER, General BENJ. PIERCE, of New Hampshire; JESSE SMITH, WILLIAM FRENCH, RUSSEL DEWEY, WM. LOW, THOMAS DAVIS, NAthaniel Rice, Amos Foster, David Brewer, Elijah Jourdan, J. Page and A. Smith—all soldiers, but to what regiments they belonged are now unknown; the nameless "army chaplain," Thomas Cooke, Hon. Wm. Tudor, Hon. John Adams, (who was then in Congress in Philadelphia,) and Judge Winthrop, none of whom were present, and in whose testimony there is not a single syllable concerning the expedition which was sent to the heights in the evening of the 16th June.

I come now to the testimony of the Connecticut troops who went out on that memorable expedition, and find that General John Keyes—who was Captain Knowlton's brother-in-law, and first Lieutenant—whose position, as the second in command, would have given unusually fine opportunities for seeing Putnam's exploits, had he done any, is equally silent respecting that officer, and he makes no allusion whatever to him in connexion with this expedition. So also were Governor Brooks, Alexander Davidson, Isaac Hunt and Francis Davidson, of Bridge's Massachusetts regiment; Philip Bagley and John Stevens, of Frye's Massachusetts regiment; and Ezra Runnels, of Gridley's (Massachusetts) artillery, all in the expedition, but equally silent about Putnam.

With these names withdrawn from "*Selah's*" alleged advocates of Putnam, there are but few left of the "all" who "agree that he (Putnam) there performed the duties devolving upon a commander;" and who, "as well as their comrades in arms, always considered him their commander." If "*Selah*" or his squire had possessed the least particle of self-respect, they would never have made this attempt to impose upon the credulity of your readers.

even in support of a bad cause; nor would they now be willing to look any honest man in the face.

As I have said, the names which I have selected above, from those referred to in "*Selah's*" letter, do not mention PUTNAM, either directly or indirectly, in connexion with the expedition now under consideration, leaving only JOSIAH CLEVELAND, JOSHUA YEOMANS, ABNER ALLEN, JOHN DEXTER and Judge GROSVENOR, of PUTNAM's Connecticut regiment, and EBENEZER BANCROFT, of BRIDGE's Massachusetts regiment, who make the least possible reference to PUTNAM as having been present, or exercising authority at that time. But, still farther, even these do not sustain "*Selah's*" assertion concerning the extent of PUTNAM's authority. CLEVELAND, YOUMANS, ALLEN and DEXTER, speak of him only as "leading" and "ordering" the Connecticut troops, of which he was the Colonel; leaving to "*Selah*" only BANCROFT and PUTNAM's son-in-law, GROSVENOR, as the sole support for his ambitious theory. As I have never denied that PUTNAM might have been present with the party, as a reference to my account of Bunker Hill (*Battles of the United States*, 1, page 52,) will show, I have no fault to find with the testimony of the four witnesses who are first named; in fact, they are more favorable to me than to "*Selah*" or his assistant. The son-in-law of PUTNAM— by no means a disinterested witness—says, "Being under the command of General PUTNAM, part of our regiment, and a much larger number of Massachusetts troops, under Colonel PRESCOTT, were ordered to march on the evening of the 16th of June, 1775, to Breed's Hill, where, under the immediate superintendence of General PUTNAM, ground was broken and a redoubt formed." The other witness, EDWARD BANCROFT, says he " was at the laying out of the works on Breed's Hill," and that "the lines were marked out by PUTNAM." On this testimony alone, added to a large amount of assertion, "*Selah*" rests his case; and with an amount of assurance which but few beside himself and his assistant can produce, he boldly proclaims that PUTNAM commanded the expedition. At the proper time I propose to inquire who commanded the troops on that eventful night, contenting myself, for the present, by citing disinterested witnesses to show that "*Selah*" and his friend are mistaken. *Deacon* SAMUEL LAWRENCE—father of ABBOTT and AMOS LAWRENCE, names with which every New Englander is familiar—made an affidavit, in which appear these words: "I, SAMUEL LAWRENCE, of Groton, Esquire, testify and say, that I was at the battle of Bunker's Hill, (so called,) in Colonel WILLIAM PRESCOTT'S regiment; that I marched with the regiment to the point on Breed's Hill, which was fixed on for a redoubt; that I assisted in throwing up the work, and in forming a redoubt, under Colonel PRESCOTT, who directed the whole of this operation. The work was begun about nine o'clock in the evening of June 16, 1775. I was there the whole time, and continued in the redoubt, or in the little fort, during the whole battle, until the enemy came in and a retreat was ordered. General PUTNAM was not present, either while the work was erecting or during the battle," &c. Mr. BANCROFT (*History of United States*, 7, page 410,) says of this event, "PUTNAM also, during the night, came among the men of Connecticut on the hill; but he assumed no command over the detachment." Mr. FROTHINGHAM, (*Siege of Boston*, 2d edition, page 122,) says, "Here (Charlestown Neck) Major BROOKS joined them, and, probably, General PUTNAM and another General;" and again, (page 124,)

"When the detachment reached Breed's Hill, the packs were thrown off, the guns were stacked, Colonel GRIDLEY marked out the plan of a fortification, tools were distributed," &c. Colonel WILLIAM PRESCOTT ("*Letter to John Adams, Camp at Cambridge,* Aug. 25, 1775,") says, "We arrived at the spot, the lines were drawn by the engineer, and we began the entrenchment," &c. Hon. WILLIAM TUDOR, son of the Judge-Advocate-General of the army, who tried some of the cowards of Bunker Hill, (*Life of Otis,* p. 469.) without alluding to PUTNAM, says, "The troops under the direction of Colonel GRIDLEY, an able engineer, were busily engaged in throwing up a small redoubt," &c. This brings me to the next branch of my inquiry.

IV. WHO WAS THE COMMANDER OF THE EXPEDITION? As has been already shown, "*Selah*" claims the honor for General PUTNAM, as he has also claimed for that officer the general command of all the "American troops" then before Boston. I have examined this latter claim, and showed that, although the orders which were issued to the Connecticut troops proceeded from him, as their senior general officer present, those under which the Massachusetts troops acted did not proceed from him, but from General WARD of Massachusetts; and I have proved therefrom that PUTNAM was not "the commander-in-chief of the American troops before the battle." Pursuing the investigation downward, I have next shown that although PUTNAM may have been present during the night of June 16th, it was not he who acted as the engineer in laying out the works; that if KEYES and other Connecticut men, and PRESCOTT and other Massachusetts men, all belonging to that expedition, are to be relied on, it was not he who commanded the expedition; and that if CLEVELAND, DEXTER, YOUMANS and ALLEN, all belonging to his own regiment, can be relied on, he may have "led" and "ordered" his own regiment, although even that is denied by many of those who are best informed on this and kindred subjects. I now propose to inquire, as PUTNAM was *not*, who *was* the commander of the expedition.

General WARD, the commander of the Massachusetts army, and President of the Council of War, who directed the movement, (*Letter to John Adams*, Oct. 30, 1775,) says, "Some have said hard things of the officers belonging to this colony (Massachusetts), but I think, as mean as they have represented them to be, there has been no one action with the enemy which has not been conducted by *an officer of this colony*, except that at Chelsea, which was conducted by General PUTNAM." General HEATH, also a member of the Council of War, (*Memoirs*, page 70,) speaking of his orders to Colonels HAND and PRESCOTT, to oppose General HOWE, on Throgg's Neck, calls PRESCOTT "*the hero of Bunker's Hill;*" Rev. JOHN MARTIN, who was in the thickest of the fight, in a communication to President STILES, "June 30, 1775," says the colonists "took possession of Bunker's Hill, under the command of Colonel PRESCOTT." Dr. JAMES THACHER, who at that time was the associate of President WARREN and others of the leading men of Massachusetts, (*Military Journal*, page 26,) says, "Orders were given to Colonel PRESCOTT, a veteran of the last war, with one thousand men, to march silently," &c. Colonel WILLIAM PRESCOTT, "the hero of Bunker's Hill," (*Letter to John Adams*, Aug. 25, 1775,) says, "On the 16th June, in the evening, *I* received orders to march to Breed's Hill, in Charlestown," &c. Hon. WM. TUDOR, son of the Judge-Advocate-General of the army, already referred to, (*Life of Otis*, page 469,) after speaking at some length of Colonel PRESCOTT, says, "On the 16th June, three regiments were placed under *him*, and *he* was ordered to Charlestown in the evening, to take possession of Bunker's Hill, and throw up works in its defense." Rev. PETER THACHER— the chairman of the sub-committee of the Massachusetts Committee of Safety, which prepared the narrative of the battle already referred to—left, appended to a copy of that narrative, in his own hand-writing, these words: "The following account was written by a person who was an eye-witness of the battle of Bunker's Hill; what facts he did not see himself were communicated to him from Colonel PRESCOTT, (*who commanded the Provincials*,)" &c. Dr. GORDON, who was then at or near Roxbury, in his invaluable history of the American Revolution, (*Ed. London*, 1788, 2, page 39,) says, "Orders were issued that a detachment of a thousand men, under Colonel WILLIAM PRESCOTT, do march at evening and entrench upon the hill," &c. Chief Justice MARSHALL, (*Life of Washington, Ed. London*, 1804, 2, page 289,) says, "In observance of these instructions, a detachment of one thousand men, under the command of General PRESCOTT, was ordered to take possession of this ground." Mr. BANCROFT, (*History of the United States*, 7, pages 408–410,) confirms this opinion, closing his remarks with the words which were cited under the last division of this subject. JAMES GRAHAM, a British authority, (*History of United States, Ed. London*, 1836, 4, p. 379,) says, "Orders were accordingly communicated to Colonel PRESCOTT, with a detachment of one thousand men, to take possession of the eminence." The able author of the article on "Bunker Hill," which appeared in the "Analectic Magazine," for Feb., 1818, after speaking of Breed's Hill, proceeds thus : "Here it was that a detachment from the American army of one thousand men, under Colonel PRESCOTT, began at 12 o'clock," &c. In that work for March, 1818, is a more minute account of this portion of the history, compiled from information received from Governor BROOKS, of Massachusetts, who, it will be remembered, was present ; in which, after describing the character of those who went out of the camp to occupy the heights, he adds, " Colonel PRESCOTT had the command." Dr. HOLMES, in his valuable "Annals of America," (*Ed. Cambridge*, 1829, 2, page 209,) says, " Orders were accordingly issued on the 16th June for a detachment of one thousand men, under Colonel PRESCOTT, to take possession of that eminence," &c. Mr. FROTHINGHAM (*Siege of Boston*, page 122,) says, " The detachment was placed under the command of Colonel WILLIAM PRESCOTT, of Pepperell, who had orders from General WARD to proceed to Bunker Hill," &c. Mr. ELLIS (*Oration at Charlestown*, 17th June, 1841, pages 27, 28,) speaks of Colonel PRESCOTT only as the commander of the expedition. Mr. EVERETT (*Oration at Charlestown*, 17th June, 1836, page 19,) says, " PRESCOTT, the Colonel of one of the Middlesex regiments, was the officer who, on the 16th June, received the orders of the Council of War to occupy the heights of Charlestown, and who commanded in the redoubt on the day of the battle." Deacon SAMUEL LAWRENCE, a soldier on the hill, in the deposition which has been cited in the last division of this subject, says, " I assisted in throwing up the work, and in forming a redoubt, under Colonel PRESCOTT, who directed the whole of this operation." Other authorities might be cited to support this assertion, were it necessary ; but I will close with inviting the attention of " *Selah* " to his friend, Colonel

SWETT, who, in his "History of Bunker's Hill Battle," third edition, page 18, tells us that, "with the advice of the Council of War, General WARD issued orders to Colonel WILLIAM PRESCOTT, Colonel BRIDGE, and the commandant of FRYE's regiment, to be prepared for an expedition, with all their men fit for service, and one day's provisions. The same order issued for one hundred and twenty of General PUTNAM's regiment, and Captain GRIDLEY's company of artillery, with two field-pieces. With these troops Colonel PRESCOTT was ordered to proceed to Charlestown in the evening, take possession of Bunker's Hill," &c. Again, on the next page, he says, "Not an officer in the army could have been selected better deserving the honor of the appointment, or more able to execute the arduous enterprise, than Colonel PRESCOTT. In this veteran, age already began to display its ravages; but the fire of his youth was undamped." Lastly, on page 20 of the same work, he says, "GRIDLEY laid out the works immediately with skill, which would honor any engineer in the highest advance of military science."

With these evidences of the unsoundness of "*Selah's*" theory of the origin, means, and direction of the expedition of the 16th of June, I submit this part of the subject to the judgment of your readers. I have never denied that PUTNAM, when present, was the commandant of his own regiment, nor do I now deny it; and I have yet to learn that in refusing to extend to him an authority which he did not possess, until some weeks afterwards, I am either injuring the reputation of PUTNAM or the "honor of Connecticut." If I may be allowed to judge, however, from cause to effect, I can easily perceive how those who seek to obtain honors for PUTNAM and for Connecticut, which belong to other men and to other States, may readily excite the alarm of others, and commit a wrong which PUTNAM, if living, would condemn, while Connecticut herself gains nothing from the controversy.

Before proceeding to an examination of the second grand division of "*Selah's*" elaborate letter, two subjects require a brief examination, not only for the confirmation of my views of the occupation of the Hill, but for the correct understanding of the truth, and of "*Selah's*" errors, on the matter of the action of the succeeding day.

I. DID PUTNAM REMAIN ON THE HEIGHTS DURING THE WHOLE OF THE NIGHT; AND IF NOT, WHY DID HE LEAVE THE EXPEDITION? Mr. FROTHINGHAM (*Siege of Boston*, page 124,) says, " General PUTNAM, after the men were at labor, returned to Cambridge." Colonel SWETT (*History of Bunker Hill Battle*, page 21,) says, " The men quietly at their labors, General PUTNAM repaired to his camp to prepare for the anticipated crisis, by bringing on reinforcements, and to be fresh mounted; his furious riding requiring a frequent change of horses." Accepting these statements as true—of which I should have no doubt, since "*Selah's*" assistant endorses them—I would respectfully inquire if it was the duty of the commander of the expedition—the part which my opponents have assigned to PUTNAM—to abandon his command, in order to seek reinforcements? and whether it was not the usual practice of "the commander-in-chief of the American troops," which dignified office "*Selah*" and his squire have claimed for PUTNAM, to employ an aid-de-camp in all such duties? I would also inquire from my Hartford friends, if this was the object of PUTNAM's mission to Cambridge, why Major BROOKS, at 9 o'clock, A. M., was sent after him on the same errand?

Why, in view of the authority with which PUTNAM is said to have been vested, *he* did not succeed in obtaining the reinforcements he went after? Why *he* was returning to the Hill, without the desired assistance—a powerless "commander-in-chief"—when Major BROOKS met him, between 9 and 10 o'clock the next morning? And, finally, why, *under these circumstances*, the latter officer, also, did *not* return to the Hill, but continued on his course to Cambridge, for the same purpose for which he had been despatched, by Colonel Prescott, from Breed's Hill? I would also most respectfully inquire from "*Selah*" and his attendant where "the furious riding" had taken place, which compelled PUTNAM to repair to Cambridge, whence the detachment had just come, for "a change of horses," as soon as "the men were quietly at work;" especially since the march from that place had been conducted with the greatest possible silence? Can my opponents also oblige me by explaining why the regiment of New Hampshire troops, under Colonel STARK, was not ordered to Charlestown by General PUTNAM, instead of by General WARD, (*Col. Stark to N. H. Committee of Safety*, June 19, 1775,) if the former held the supreme command? These questions are all pertinent to the issue, and "*Selah*" may enlighten me, and possibly himself, by ascertaining and communicating the true answers, with references to his authorities. I will not trouble him to copy the authorities at length, as, notwithstanding I live in the country, I presume I have the works on my shelves.

11. HOW WAS GENERAL PUTNAM EMPLOYED FROM THE TIME HE LEFT THE MEN AT WORK, IN THE NIGHT OF JUNE 16TH, TO THE OPENING OF THE ENGAGEMENT ON THE FOLLOWING AFTERNOON? As has been shown, "General PUTNAM,

after the men were at labor, returned to Cambridge." As it was "about twelve o'clock" when "the men began to work," (*Frothingham*, page 124; *Swett*, page 21; *Bancroft*, 7, page 409; *Thacher's Military Journal*, page 26,) and as the General was mounted (*Swett*, page 21,) it could not have been later than one o'clock when the latter reached his camp; so that from and after one o'clock in the morning of June 17th, until the commencement of the action, on the afternoon of the same day, is the period of time which is now under consideration. The most zealous friend of PUTNAM makes no pretense that he did anything after he arrived at Cambridge, (about one o'clock,) until daybreak—about four o'clock—when, it is said, he "directed Lieutenant CLARK to send to General WARD for a horse;" and of this no contemporary evidence is adduced, nor does any appear, in the numerous affidavits and letters which the long-continued discussion on Bunker Hill has drawn forth. Admitting, therefore, the truth of Colonel SWETT's assertion, for the argument's sake, not less than three hours of that eventful night were spent by PUTNAM, "*Selah's*" incomparable commander-in-chief, in his camp at Cambridge, in some private, untold occupation—"preparing for the anticipated crisis," it is said; while PRESCOTT and KNOWLTON and their men, in a different style, were also "preparing" for that event, with spade and pick-axe and crow-bar, within the lines on the heights of Charlestown. History has recorded the determined, uncompromising patriotism of the latter; and the story of their zeal, their sufferings and their bravery, will go down to future ages with constantly increasing glory; while generations yet unborn will associate the names of WARREN and PRESCOTT, KNOWLTON and STARK, with the great principles for which they fought ; and in giving thanks for the blessings with which they will be surrounded, they will not forget to mention those through whose instrumentality they have been secured.

I have said that Colonel SWETT—" *Selah's* " great leader —states that " at day-break, PUTNAM directed Lieutenant CLARK to send to General WARD for a horse ;" but the Colonel, and " *Selah* " after him, wisely declined to draw the curtain, and show the whereabouts and occupation of PUTNAM from one to four o'clock on that morning. Without doing more than pointing out to your readers the peculiar situation of PUTNAM at day-break, compared with that of PRESCOTT at the same moment, I might rest my case, and safely leave to their judgment the determination of the matter at issue. On the one hand, we have the " tall and commanding " figure of PRESCOTT, with " countenance grave, ardent and impressive as his character ;" " and, with his formidable sword, he needed no uniform to distinguish him as a *leader*" (*Swett's Bunker Hill Battle*, page 19.) " In a simple calico frock he had headed the detachment which left camp at dark " (*Ibid.*) ; and now, with " these brawney yeomen," " instructing and stimulating " them, he was " working for their lives as well as their liberties," on Breed's Hill ; or, " watchful as Argus," was cautiously providing for their safety (*Swett*, page 21). On the other hand, we have PUTNAM, a " rugged son of Mars," (*Ibid.*, page 7,) the assumed " director and superintendent of the expedition," (*Ibid.*, 19,)

" Turning his sides, his shoulders, and his heavy head,"

in his camp at Cambridge, several miles distant from the men of whom he is claimed to have been the " director," and of the works of which, in that case, he would have been the " superintendent." Like a prudent man, he had left the scene of danger, his men and the works, three hours before, in order that he might " prepare for the anticipated crisis," by securing, in a safe place, a comfortable nap. The guns of the *Lively*, which had just opened their fire on the works which PUTNAM had *not* " superintended," and on the men whom he had *not* " directed," at the time in question, had aroused " the American Samson" (*Swett*, page 6,) (as they had also aroused General GAGE in Boston,) from the slumbers into which he had fallen ; and he hastened to complete the " preparations," which had been so successfully commenced. At once, therefore, rubbing open his eyes, and unrolling himself from the blanket in which, for three hours, he had been " preparing for the anticipated crisis," the glorious " commander-in-chief," like Richard of old, could only cry out, in his confusion,

" A horse, a horse, my kingdom for a horse!"

before he returned to his slumbers ; and, for five hours more, he was as busily occupied in completing his " preparations," before leaving the camp, on his return to the hill.*
As I said before, like a prudent man, he had sought safety and comfort in Cambridge ; your readers, Mr. Editor, can judge, therefrom, of his qualifications for the post of " commander-in-chief of the American forces, before the battle," as well as of the true character and extent of his authority on Breed's Hill.

But to proceed. Colonel SWETT says that "at daybreak," PUTNAM was at Cambridge, calling for a horse ; and that

---

* He was met on Charlestown Neck by Major Brooks, at between nine and ten o'clock in the morning—his first appearance—on the 17th of June.

he "flew to join his men on the hill," (page 24.) Strange to say, however, not a single soldier has been found who was willing to swear he saw him there *after* the *Lively* opened her fire, at which time he had not left Cambridge; nor can one be found who will venture to say anything about him, until between 9 and 10 o'clock. more than four hours later, when Major Brooks, then on his way to Cambridge to ask for reinforcements, met him on the Neck, riding toward the hill. In the absence of any corroborative testimony on this subject, "*Selah*" must pardon me for the rejection of Colonel Swett's assertion that Putnam visited the works before 10 o'clock. I have no doubt that "*Selah*" has good reasons for endorsing the trustworthiness of that venerable friend of Putnam; I have reasons, which are satisfactory to myself, at least, for rejecting everything which he says on Putnam. unless it is supported by other and better authorities. I cannot forget that this gentleman, for party purposes, in order to influence a popular election for Governor of Massachusetts, embarked in a Putnam crusade, "devoting two months of his life, night and day, to this subject;"* and that, with all the malignity of party spirit, immediately after the close of the last war with Great Britain, he gathered, garbled and published the testimony to which "*Selah*" refers. I cannot forget that it was he who, in 1818, edited an edition of "Humphrey's Life of Putnam," with an appendix, on page 212 of which he gravely asserted that Putnam remained on the hill all night,† notwithstanding the contrary was proved by

---

* "The reviewer should devote two months of his life, night and day, to this subject, as the author has, before he makes his strictures with such overweening confidence."— Col. *Swett to Ballard & Wright, in answer to* "*L.,*" 1818.

† "The men quietly at their labors, Gen. Putnam, *in the morning*, repaired to the

the testimony which he possessed at the time;* nor do I fail to remember that he was compelled to correct that statement in subsequent editions.† He it was, too, who mutilated the depositions of REUBEN KEMP and ALEXANDER DAVIDSON, and the statements of Judge-Advocate TUDOR, and the Hon. Mr. COOKE, of Doctor JAMES THACHER, Colonel SARGENT of New Hampshire, and the Rev. JOHN MARTIN, compelling them to appear in the character of witnesses *for* PUTNAM, while they really testified against his claims; and when, in this connexion, the fact is borne in mind that the strongest testimony which "*Selah*" produces, in support of PUTNAM'S pretensions, are depositions of soldiers who had been influenced by fees and gifts, at the expense of the Federalists of Boston, for the purpose of defeating General DEARBORN; that they were made by men, a great number of whom could not sign their own names, or read for themselves, what others had written for them; and that they were prepared and verified in the presence of only one party, for the use of that party only the amount of credibility which attaches to Colonel SWETT's unsupported assertions will be readily perceived, and some of the reasons for my rejection of all such testimony as unworthy of the name of history.

If PUTNAM was on the hill between one and ten o'clock, it appears strange that no testimony has yet been found to

---

camp to prepare for the anticipated crisis," &c.—*Sketch of Bunker Hill Battle, in App. to Humphrey's Putnam,* 1818.

* "*At day-break*, Gen. Putnam ordered Lieut. Clark to send and request of Gen. Ward a horse for him *to ride to Bunker Hill.*"—*The same work, page* 217.

† Without attempting to reconcile the inconsistency of his remarks, that Putnam remained on the Hill "*until morning*," although he was said to have been at Cambridge "*at day-break*," in the third edition of the "*Sketch,*" (page 21) Col. Swett has omitted the words "*in the morning*" from the description of Putnam's departure from the Hill.

prove it; and if he was at Cambridge during those hours, or during any portion of the same period, what was he doing there? The "preparations" which he had made during that time have received no notice, even from his most particular friends; and all that we know of his movements, during the nine hours which he was absent from the hill, was the visit which he made to Prospect Hill, "early in the morning," to order DOOLITTLE's regiment to march to the Hill "by 9 o'clock," (*Deposition of Captain John Holden, Adjutant of the day,*) which, being composed of Massachusetts men, it did not obey—Major MOORE, who commanded the regiment, having joined the troops who had thrown up the works, "just previous to the action," (*Frothingham*, page 136; *Swett's Bunker Hill Battle*, page 30; *Bancroft*, 7, page 418), and then only as volunteers, or under orders from General WARD, who alone was his legal commander.

He reached the works, then, about ten o'clock, and busied himself in attempting to find men who would obey his orders, and throw up some defensive works on Bunker's Hill. In this undertaking—a very proper one at that time—he appears to have met the same resolute disobedience which had troubled him before; and at eleven o'clock, when Doctor THOMAS KITTREDGE left the Hill, PUTNAM was at the foot of Bunker's Hill, requesting some of the by-standers to go to the fort, and see if they could get some of the intrenching tools, (Dr. KITTREDGE's *Deposition.*) General BENJAMIN PIERCE, of New Hampshire, (father of ex-President PIERCE), also saw PUTNAM about 11 o'clock on Bunker's Hill, (*Deposition of General Pierce.*) At a later hour—during which interval we find no mention of his whereabouts in any contemporary document or authority—

he went *in person,* "and told Colonel PRESCOTT that the intrenching tools must be sent off, or they would be lost; the Colonel replied, that if he sent any of the men away with the tools, not one of them would return; to this the General answered, 'they shall every man return.' A large party was then sent off with the tools, and not one of them returned." (*General Heath's Memoirs,* p. 20.) With this party, increased by others, who, like himself, preferred to be more distant from danger than the positions which PRESCOTT and KNOWLTON occupied, PUTNAM returned to Bunker's Hill, and there he remained, with but little, if any interruption, until the action commenced. Among the earliest of the reinforcements which reached the peninsula was Colonel GERRISH's regiment, one of whose men, WILLIAM MARDEN, says that on reaching the top of Bunker's Hill, he saw General PUTNAM on horseback, riding backward and forward, urging the men onward to the charge, and presently saw him ride down the hill toward the works, (*Deposition of William Marden.*) Colonel STARK's regiment came up about two o'clock—having left Medford, four miles distant, "about one o'clock"—and, "as it passed on to Breed's Hill," when near the summit of Bunker's Hill, General PUTNAM was seen "on the declivity towards Charlestown Neck, with Colonel GERRISH by his side." (*Statement of General Henry Dearborn.*) Major CALEB STARK, of the same regiment, (*Letter to General Wilkinson,* Nov., 1815,) says, "His (PUTNAM's) station was on Bunker Hill, and he performed *no portion* of the operations at Breed's Hill." REUBEN KEMP, of the same regiment, also speaks of the work on *Bunker's* Hill, as well as other subjects connected with the action, which will be noticed in their proper places. (*Deposition of Reuben Kemp.*) That portion of Colonel BRIDGE's regiment which Captain FORD commanded, "reached the Hill just before the action began," (*Frothingham*, p. 176,) yet even then PUTNAM was on *Bunker's* Hill.—"As we were going on to the lines, and had gained the hill *back of Breed's Hill*, General PUTNAM came up to Captain FORD, and told him that two pieces were left," &c. (*Deposition of Alexander Davidson, of Ford's Company*.) General BENJAMIN PIERCE, (father of ex-President PIERCE,) who also served in FORD's Company, says, "PUTNAM did not give any orders, or assume any command, except on *Bunker's Hill, as they were going to the field of battle.*" (*General Pierce's deposition.*) Colonel MOSES LITTLE, at the head of three of his companies, marched to the hill, and took their station on the right of the breast-work, immediately before the battle commenced, (*Frothingham*, p. 177; *Deposition of Benjamin Webber,*) and WEBBER, one of his men, a friend of General PUTNAM, says, and swears to it, that "passing over *Bunker's* Hill, we saw General PUTNAM, who rode up to Captain WARNER, and said, "My brave fellows, march forward to the breastwork on Breed's Hill," (*Deposition of Benjamin Webber.*) Captain JAMES CLARK, of PUTNAM's regiment—one of our hero's own officers—says, that while he was crossing Charlestown Neck, the firing commenced, and that, at the same time, he saw General PUTNAM on horseback, at, or near the same place. Captain TREVETT, of GRIDLEY's artillery, also "arrived on *Bunker's* Hill, and saw General PUTNAM; halted, and went forward to select a station for his company; returned, and saw PUTNAM in the *same* place as before. *At this time* the action had commenced." (*Deposition of Captain Trevett.*)

I need not pursue this branch of my inquiry any farther,

although an abundant supply of material yet remains unemployed. Your readers will perceive that I have used but few witnesses who had not already been introduced to their notice by "*Selah*" and his assistant, in their last communication; and I take pleasure in referring to the fact that they embrace men of the highest character in their respective regiments. From this testimony—and there is none which can contradict it with any force—it is clear that PUTNAM was asleep in his tent, or otherwise withdrawn from public life, until the guns of the *Lively* aroused the entire army near five o'clock on the 17th; that from that time until about nine o'clock, he was riding about the encampments, seeking for some Massachusetts or New Hampshire regiment, which would receive his orders and march to the Hill, in which he found that none were so mean as to do *him* reverence; that about nine he started toward the Hill, meeting Major BROOKS, and that he reached Bunker's Hill soon afterward; that he again renewed his effort to find a command, in which, after securing the aid of the venerable POMEROY, (*Deposition of William French,*) he so far succeeded, that Colonel PRESCOTT was deprived of the greater part of his force; that with these, and such poltroons as GERRISH, he commenced to throw up a breast-work on *Bunker's* Hill; that he was on that Hill immediately before the action commenced; and that he was on the declivity of the same Hill, toward the Neck, or on the Neck itself, at the moment when the action commenced, on the other side the Hill.

This brings me to the second grand division of my opponents' communication—THE PART WHICH PUTNAM PERFORMED IN THE ENGAGEMENT OF THE 17TH JUNE. In this, as in other branches of the subject through which I have passed,

I propose to separate the examination of each part from that of the others, not only for my own convenience, but for that of your readers in following me through the confusion into which the party hacks, forty years ago, have thrown this simple historical subject. To my own satisfaction, at least, I have directed the attention of your readers to the occupation of PUTNAM, on the 17th of June, 1775, before the commencement of the action; and I now proceed to inquire:

I. IN WHAT MANNER WAS HE ENGAGED, AND WHERE WAS HE DURING THE FIRST ATTACK BY THE ENEMY? It will be remembered the enemy landed at Morton's Point, on the eastern extremity of the peninsula on which Breed's and Bunker's Hills are situated, (*Swett,* p. 26,) that this point is upwards of nine hundred yards, *in a straight line,* from the redoubt and the rail-fence, while that portion of Charlestown Neck which is nearest to the works on Breed's Hill and to the rail-fence, is not less than the same distance, in a direct line, from the scene of the action, (*Map in Swett's History, and the scale on it.*) It will also be remembered that the rail-fence was from one hundred and ninety to two hundred yards distant from the entrenchments, at the points where they most nearly approached each other, (*Frothingham,* p. 135; *Swett,* p. 27;) that this position was occupied by Captain KNOWLTON, *after* the enemy had landed at Morton's Point, (*Frothingham,* p. 134; *Swett,* p. 26,) and that the period of time embraced in the first attack on the works—that is, from the first fire, on either side, to the flight of the assailants—did not exceed five minutes.

With these facts before us to start with, let us examine the evidence, and inquire "where PUTNAM was, and what he was doing, during these eventful five minutes?" The testimony already adduced shows that a few minutes before the action began, he was on *Bunker's* Hill, between the redoubt and Charlestown Neck, and his own most ardent friends have never asserted the contrary. Captain JAMES CLARK, of PUTNAM's Connecticut regiment, was on Charlestown Neck when the firing commenced, and PUTNAM, on horseback, was at or in sight from that place, as Captain CLARK "saw General PUTNAM as he was crossing the Neck," which would seem impossible—Bunker's Hill intervening—if PUTNAM had been on or near the scene of the action. Captain TREVETT, of GRIDLEY's artillery, in the deposition already cited, testifies that PUTNAM was on the north-west side of Bunker's Hill, toward the Neck, and opposite from the scene of action, while "the action was then going on." I cite this from Colonel SWETT's synopsis of the deposition. (*Notes, &c.*, p. 8.) Deacon MILLER, also an ensign in Colonel GARDNER's regiment, "said, repeatedly, that he saw PUTNAM on *Bunker's* Hill when the action commenced." SAMUEL BASSETT, of STYLE's company, STARK's regiment, left the camp after the regiment had marched, and testifies that he "arrived at Ploughed Hill, near the Neck," (now Mount Benedict, on the main land.) "a few minutes before the fire commenced. In about fifteen minutes, General PUTNAM came up on the gallop, and said, "Up, my brave boys, for God's sake; we drive them." (*Deposition of Samuel Bassett.*)

As, by the testimony previously adduced, it has been shown that, before the battle, PUTNAM, with the coward GERRISH, occupied the north-west slope of Bunker's Hill, out of harm's way, so, by the positive testimony of eye-witnesses—Captains CLARK and TREVETT, Ensign MILLER and STEPHEN BASSETT—it is quite as certainly shown that he remained there during the first attack, and until he rode over the Neck toward Cambridge, with the intelligence of the repulse of the enemy. It is true that, for political purposes, REUBEN KEMP, of STARK's regiment, has sworn that he was posted, with his company, " at the redoubt and breastwork, which was thrown up the night before ;" that they " remained there till the enemy came to the attack;" and that " General PUTNAM seemed to have the ordering of things," &c. It is equally true, however, that garbled and mutilated copies of this deposition, changing its character, have been circulated by the friends of PUTNAM to support a bad cause ; (*compare Colonel Swett's Notes, pages 4, 5, with the original,*) that STARK's regiment was not posted in the works " which was thrown up the night before," as KEMP pretends, but at the rail-fence, near the Mystic river, (*General Dearborn's letter to the Portfolio,* page 175,) and that Judge WINTHROP, of Cambridge, Judge ABEL PARKER, of New Hampshire, and Deacon LAWRENCE, of Groton—father of Hon. ABBOTT LAWRENCE— all of whom were present, testify positively that PUTNAM was not in that part of the field.

It is also true that ISAAC BASSETT, of PUTNAM's regiment, testifies that he, too, " arrived at the redoubt and breastwork just before the battle began, and saw General PUTNAM there encouraging the troops," &c. It is equally true, however, that all the Connecticut troops were with KNOWLTON at the rail-fence, (*Swett,* page 26 ; *Frothingham,* page 134,) instead of being at the redoubt and breastwork; that the evidence of those who were at the latter works positively disprove the statement ; and that another witness in the same cause—ALEXANDER DAVIDSON—asserts positively that at the same time he is said to have been on the Hill, he was present behind the rail-fence, near the Mystic.

But, as if to prove the frailty of all that is human, General PUTNAM himself has settled the question, as the following extract from President STILES' MS. *Diary*—that valuable receptacle of the current news of the day—will fully prove:

"JUNE 23, 1775.—Messrs. ELLERY, CHANG, &c., returned here from a visit to the camp, which they left on Saturday last. They spent an hour with General PUTNAM in his tent on Prospect Hill, about half-way between Cambridge and Charlestown. The General gave them an account of the battle last Saturday, said the number on one side was not ascertained," &c.

"PUTNAM *was not at Bunker Hill at the beginning, but soon repaired thither*, and was in the heat of the action till toward night, when he went away to fetch across this reinforcement, which ought to have come before. Soon after, and before he could return, our men began to retreat," &c.

As the entry speaks of "our body on *Bunker* Hill, where was the action"—the place at which "PUTNAM was *not* at the beginning"—it will be perfectly apparent to all that reference is here made to the scene of that action of which "*Selah*" and his squire, following Colonel SWETT and the Federalists of 1818, would have the people of Connecticut believe ISRAEL PUTNAM was the commander-in-chief and the hero.

Having shown that General PUTNAM was not present during the first attack of the enemy on the Colonists, let us inquire:

II. IN WHAT MANNER WAS HE ENGAGED, AND WHERE WAS HE, BETWEEN THE FIRST AND SECOND ATTACKS ON THE AMERI-

CAN WORKS? In answer to this question, I need only submit the statements of "*Selah's*" own witnesses. DANIEL PUTNAM, the General's son, in his letter of Oct. 19, 1825, says, "In the interval between the first and second attacks of the British on our line, he (General PUTNAM) rode back to Bunker Hill, and in the rear of it, to urge on reinforcements." This statement is confirmed by Colonel SWETT, (pages 35-6,) and by Mr. FROTHINGHAM, (*Siege of Boston*, pages 142-3,) and, as all parties appear to agree on this point—that PUTNAM was not on the field of battle between the first and second attacks of the enemy—I need not occupy your columns by unnecessarily enlarging on the subject. I proceed, therefore, to inquire:

III. IN WHAT MANNER WAS HE ENGAGED, AND WHERE WAS HE, DURING THE SECOND ATTACK ON THE WORKS BY THE ENEMY? After a careful examination of all the authorities—those which support, as well as those which oppose, the pretensions of General PUTNAM's friends—I have been unable to find any one which pretends that the General was on the field of battle during the second attack. He had started off towards Cambridge, under the pretense of bringing forward the reinforcements; and when he was near Charlestown Neck, he met Colonel GARDNER's regiment, (*Depositions of Enoch Baldwin, Deacon Miller, and others belonging to that regiment*,) and ordered it to go to work on the entrenchment on *Bunker's* Hill, (*Depositions of E. Baldwin and Deacon Miller*.) As this regiment had walked from the main land since the first attack had been commenced, (*Depositions of William Dickson, Enoch Baldwin, and Mr. Thompson*,) and as the firing was renewed, (the second attack) just after the regiment had crossed the Neck, (*Depositions of Deacon Miller, William Dickson, and Captain*

Francis Green,) where Putnam met it; and as PUTNAM, with this regiment, *was on the top of Bunker's Hill,* while the action was still going on below, (*Deposition of William Dickson,*) I can readily account for the silence of those who would gladly have given their hero this honor, if it could have been done with safety. I do not forget, however, that, years ago, an attempt was made by " *Selah's* " great authority, in view of the break in his finely wrought chain of evidence, which this awkward fact produces, to repair the defect by boldly mutilating the deposition of ALEXANDER DAVIDSON; that the mutilation was detected and exposed by one of his own townsmen;* and that he acknowledged his guilt in subsequent editions of his work, by transferring his story from the second to the first attack, to which it truly applied, if it applied at all. It is by such leger-de-main as this that PUTNAM's reputation has been manufactured, from the night when the fox robbed his hen-roost, or the wolf robbed his sheep and goat pasture, to that on which he became a "skinner," and, himself, robbed the Robinson House and its vicinity, at the expense of the United States.†

I proceed, however, to inquire:

IV. WHERE WAS GENERAL PUTNAM, AND HOW WAS HE ENGAGED, BETWEEN THE SECOND AND THIRD ATTACKS ON THE AMERICAN LINES? In this, as in the last division of my subject, there is not a single friend of General PUTNAM who has pretended that he was on the field of action during the period of time embraced between the second and third attacks of the enemy. Even Colonel SWETT is silent on this

---

* David Lee Childs, Esq., in *An Inquiry into the Conduct of Gen. Israel Putnam.*
† Gen. Geo. Clinton to Col. Alex. Hamilton, Dec. 28, 1777.

subject; and "*Selah*," like all similar creatures, in similar cases, also keeps his mouth shut. ENOCH BALDWIN tells us, however, "General PUTNAM rode up to the Colonel, (GARDNER) and advised him to let his men carry some entrenching tools, and said we should not have any more fighting, as the British had been beaten twice, and had retreated the second time." (*Deposition taken by his son and Colonel Swett.*) The same *Bunker's* Hill was still the scene of his assiduous care; and while PRESCOTT and KNOWLTON and STARK were struggling with the enemy, on *Breed's* Hill and on the bank of the Mystic, PUTNAM was "advising" Colonel GARDNER, (commanders-in-chief do not " advise " their men, but " order " them,) to " carry some entrenching tools "—" advice " which the Colonel, who was more disposed to fight than to dig trenches, very speedily disregarded, by ordering his command to Colonel PRESCOTT's assistance, and by laying his own life on the altar of his country, when the enemy advanced, a third time, against the works.

Again, in this division of my subject, let me inquire:

V. WHERE WAS GENERAL PUTNAM, AND HOW WAS HE EMPLOYED, WHILE THE ENEMY WAS MAKING HIS LAST ATTACK ON THE LINES? In this also, as in the last section, the friends of PUTNAM make no claim in his behalf; but in this, as in that, there is ample testimony, among their own witnesses, from which an answer to my question may be gathered without their assistance. JESSE SMITH swears: " Was at the rail-fence; fired sixteen rounds; went off to get his musket fixed. Going up *Bunker's* Hill, saw Colonel GARDNER wounded, and General PUTNAM on his horse, urging the men *there down* to the line of battle; returning to the line, the retreat began." (*Deposition of Jesse Smith.*) Rev.

Daniel Chaplin, D.D., of Groton, and Rev. John Bullard, of Pepperell, swear that they "were intimate with Colonel Prescott; that he told us repeatedly that when the retreat was ordered and commenced, and he was descending the hill, he met General Putnam, and said to him, 'Why did not you support me, General, with your men, as I had reason to expect, according to agreement?' Putnam answered, 'I could not *drive* the dogs.' Prescott pointedly said to him, 'If you could not drive them up, you might have *led* them up.'" (*Depositions of Rev. Daniel Chaplin, D.D., and Rev. John Bullard.*) It will be seen that Putnam had been on *Bunker's* Hill during the action, and was *then* approaching Breed's Hill; and as Colonel Prescott had been the last to leave the redoubt, it will be obvious that the retreat was ordered before Putnam left his favorite post on Bunker's Hill. Robert B. Wilkins swears that "just before the retreat from the fort, I passed on to *Bunker* Hill, where I found Putnam and Gerrish again." (*Deposition of Robert B. Wilkins, of Concord.*) Captain Trevett, of the artillery, swears: "Arrived at the rail-fence when the retreat commenced; descending northwest side of *Bunker* Hill, saw General Putnam in the same place, putting his tent on his horse." (*Deposition of Captain S. R. Trevett.*) Other affidavits, were they necessary, might be cited to show that Putnam was on *Bunker's* Hill during this last attack; and that, when the retreat began, he was still on that position.

VI. What was Putnam's position during the retreat? Colonel Swett, (page 47) speaking of the troops behind the rail-fence, says: "Putnam covered their retreat with his Connecticut troops and others just arrived, and, in the rear of the whole, dared the utmost fury of the enemy, who pursued with little ardor, but poured in their thundering volleys, and showers of balls fell like hail around the General. He addressed himself to every passion of the troops, to persuade them to rally, to throw up his works on Bunker's Hill, and make a stand there, and threatened them with the eternal disgrace of deserting their General. He took his stand near a field-piece, and seemed resolved to brave the foe alone. His troops, however, felt it impossible to withstand the overwhelming force of the British bayonets; they left him. One sergeant only dared to stand by his General to the last; he was shot down, and the enemy's bayonets were just upon the General, when he retired."

Such is fancy let loose. The facts are these: "When the troops (from the fence) arrived at the summit of Bunker's Hill, we found General PUTNAM, with nearly as many men as had been engaged in the battle; notwithstanding which, no measures had been taken for reinforcing us, nor was there a shot fired to cover our retreat, or any movement made to check the advance of the enemy to this height; but, on the contrary, General PUTNAM rode off with a number of spades and pickaxes in his hands," &c. (*Narrative of General Henry Dearborn.*) SIMEON NOYES testifies that "when we were retreating, he rode up to us with his tent and tent-poles on his horse, and asked why we were retreating? He said we had been wishing to have the enemy come out, and now we had retreated, and had left the tools to fortify with; that we ought to be ashamed of such conduct. But our officers thought he was too fiery, and refused to go back as he wished." (*Deposition of Simeon Noyes.*) As these troops "had left the tools" which PUTNAM had taken up to the summit of

Bunker's Hill, it is evident they had reached the *north-west* slope of that Hill, at least, when they saw PUTNAM, and held this conversation with him.* They had passed over the Hill in their retreat, and "left the tools," which he also had left in his hurry to remove his tent and tent-poles, and, like General DEARBORN, they saw "no movement made to check the advance of the enemy," nor even "a shot fired to cover their retreat." The only tent and tent-poles which the record of those times show to have been on the peninsula, on the 17th June, were PUTNAM's; and when he found that circumstances would not permit him to seek shelter from the rays of the sun, under the folds of that tent, while he hurried up the idlers of his command, he packed it up, and removed it to a place of safety. Colonel WADE also testifies: "On the retreat, I saw PUTNAM on *Bunker's* Hill; there were entrenching tools there, and he tried to stop our troops to throw up works there." (*Deposition of Colonel Wade.*) Here also is a full confirmation of the statements of DEARBORN and NOYES; the same denial of PUTNAM's activity in covering the retreat; the same ignorance of the proximity of those terrible British bayonets to the General's breast; the same positive denial that he was on the field of battle. But this is not all: Captain FRANCIS GREEN testifies, in like manner: "On our retreat, saw PUTNAM on *Bunker's* Hill; he was in danger from the balls flying there; he tried to stop us, and to make us take up entrenching tools, as I understood him, to throw up a breastwork there." And finally, as if to scatter "*Selah's*" pretensions beyond the

---

* It will be seen that this was the identical spot on which he was when Captain Trevett, of the artillery, saw him, after the retreat had commenced.—Vide *Capt. S. R. Trevett's Deposition*, page 150.

possibility of a doubt, Judge GROSVENOR, with the full approval of PUTNAM's son, says: "They (the enemy) made a direct advance on the redoubt, and, being successful, which our brave Captain KNOWLTON perceiving, ordered a retreat of his men, in which he was sustained by two companies under the command of Captains CLARK and CHESTER," (*Judge Grosvenor to Colonel Daniel Putnam, April* 30, 1818, and published by the latter in his reply to General DEARBORN.) There are several other depositions to the same effect, of which copies can be given, should "*Selah*" or "the people of Connecticut" desire them. I imagine, however, that the character of the gentlemen already cited, and that of their testimony, will render this unnecessary.

In my last letter I referred your readers to every contemporary authority—not merely hearsay witnesses—including all who knew of that which they wrote, to disprove "*Selah's*" fictions; and I need not occupy your columns, at the present time, by citing more than the names and dates of their testimony:—The Provincial Congress of Massachusetts, by whose orders the peninsula was occupied, June 20 and June 28, 1775; the Committee of Safety of Massachusetts, July 25, 1775; Captain ELIJAH HIDE, of Lebanon, Conn., who witnessed the action, 1775; Governor JONATHAN TRUMBULL, of Connecticut, PUTNAM's superior, August 31, 1779; General FOLSOM, commander of the New Hampshire troops, June 22, 1775; ISAAC LOTHROP, in the Army, June 22, 1775; Governor JOHN BROOKS, who was on the hill, 1775; General JOHN STARK, the hero of Bennington, June 22, 1775;[*] Captain JOHN CHESTER, of

---

[*] While the "galley-proofs" of this page were before me, for correction, I received from my valued friend, CALEB STARK, Esq.—grandson of the hero of the rail-fence at Bunker's Hill, and of Bennington—a mass of most interesting manuscripts, relating,

Connecticut, with KNOWLTON behind the rail-fence, July 22, 1775; PETER BROWN, in the redoubt with PRESCOTT June 25, 1775; SAMUEL GRAY, also in the battle, July 12, 1775; Colonel WILLIAM PRESCOTT, "the hero of Bunker Hill," Aug. 25, 1775; Chief-Justice MARSHALL, 1804; Major-General HENRY LEE, of the Revolutionary army; Mrs. MERCY WARREN, a sister of JAMES OTIS and the wife of JAMES WARREN; Colonel JAMES REED, who fought behind the rail-fence, 1776; General HEATH, the first and the last General on duty in the Revolutionary army, 1798; Rev. JOHN MARTIN, who fought on the hill, and whose testimony has been mutilated by Colonel SWETT, 1775; Hon. JOHN PITTS, July 20, 1775; Dr. JAMES THACHER, of the Revolutionary army; Hon. WILLIAM TUDOR, who tried Colonel GERRISH, and some others who had faltered in the action; and Rev. Dr. GORDON, the historian, then at Roxbury—while Lieutenant CLARKE, of the British Marines, who fought in the action, also bears testimony to the incorrectness of "*Selah's*" statements.*

Finally, "*Selah*" appeals to the good opinions which General WASHINGTON and General JOSEPH REED expressed toward General PUTNAM, to disprove my remarks on this general subject, and to ward off that terrible blow which my reference to the correspondence between General

in part, to the *peculiar* "*services*" of PUTNAM, in the French War, under Colonel ROGERS, as well as to those which he did *not* perform on Breed's Hill. I regret that they did not come at an earlier date; but, with others, even more interesting than these, relating to his sympathy with the Royal cause, they have been carefully preserved for future use.

* I am indebted to the Rev. Dr. CHAPIN, of New York, for the use of Lieut. CLARKE's "*Narrative of the Battle*," &c., (London, 1775,) on the 19th page of which, after speaking of Dr. WARREN, he says: "He was supposed to be the Commander of the American army that day; for General PUTNAM was about three miles distant, *and formed an ambuscade with about three thousand men.*"

WASHINGTON and ROBERT R. LIVINGSTON inflicted on the character of General Putnam.* It affords me pleasure to meet my friend "*Selah*" on a platform such as this which he has constructed; and I beg his attention while I turn

---

* Since the publication of these letters, I have been favored with the following copies of other portions of this correspondence, *collated with the originals*, which I have considered worthy a place in these pages:

EXTRACT OF A LETTER FROM ROBT. R. LIVINGSTON TO GEN. WASHINGTON.

"Manor of Livingston, 12th January, 1778.

"Your Excellency is fully impressed with the importance of fortifying Hudson's River. The want of men and money must make this work go on very slowly, or, indeed, by leaving all unfinished, waste what shall be expended.

"Your Excellency is not ignorant of the extent of General PUTNAM's capacity and diligence; and how well soever these may qualify him for the management of this work and the command of this most important post, the unfavorable sentiments entertained of him by the people of this and the neighboring State will destroy his utility. *Of the* DISAFFECTION *with which the* POPULACE BRAND HIM—*from the intercourse which he suffers to be kept up with the enemy—from the unbounded lenity with which he trusts the disaffected*—the more thinking among us readily acquit him. But I am sorry to say, there are very few that do not charge the loss of Fort Montgomery to his *negligence*, as well as the subsequent ravages of the country on the east side of the river, which it is supposed might have been protected from an enemy who moved slowly and acted with the utmost timidity, nor ever ventured on shore but when they were sure of meeting with little or no opposition. But, sir, I will not anticipate what a future enquiry cannot fail to discover. Having the highest respect for General PUTNAM's bravery and former activity, I sincerely lament that his love for his country will not permit him to take that repose to which his advanced age and former services justly entitle him. My object in this is to hint to your Excellency the necessity of putting this department under the command of *an active and judicious officer*, of pressing Congress to furnish it with money, without which it is utterly impossible to carry on any public works with spirit, and of recommending the allowance of additional pay to soldiers employed in erecting defences on the river, as some compensation for their labor and the wear of their clothing—and to induce them to work with spirit.

"A chain and cannon will be wanting: sixteen or eighteen twelve-pounders may be got at Salisbury; in mounting these and procuring others, no time is to be lost in setting the forges at work. There are other subjects on which I could wish to address your Excellency, of no less importance to the cause of America; but this, and my fear of trespassing upon your time, induces me to defer till some future opportunity; in the meanwhile, I flatter myself that your Excellency will not only excuse, but consider the freedom with which this is written, as a new proof of the confidence which I have ever found myself inclined to repose in your Excellency, and which you have, by your goodness, so frequently encouraged, as to persuade me that I run no other hazard in speaking with equal freedom of men and measures, than that of sometimes trying your patience. We have various accounts from New York, of their being in continual

over the records, and show "the people of Connecticut" who it is I am "assailing," and what manner of man it is of whom "*Selah*" and his squire are the self-constituted defenders.

alarm, least they should receive an unwelcome visit from us during the winter. I suppose their apprehensions will be somewhat allayed by the arrival of the Seventy-first and three Hessian regiments, which have lately got in from the Delaware.

"I have the honor to be, with the greatest respect and esteem, &c.,

"ROBERT R. LIVINGSTON."

EXTRACT OF A LETTER FROM ROBT. R. LIVINGSTON TO GOUV. MORRIS.

"Rhinebeck, 29th January, 1778.

"DEAR MORRIS:—The fortifications of the river, for which no one step is yet taken of any importance. Congress have passed resolutions, they have entrusted the execution of them to General GATES, and in the same breath they have recalled him. Upon what principles do they act? Do they mean to show the world that they know the importance of that river, and at the same time that they are indifferent about its security? Or *do they mean that a work of such magnitude should be left to a man* WHOSE VERY FIDELITY IS SUSPECTED, *whose ignorance is notorious, and whose negligence has already endangered this State*. Because he is unfit to command a division of the grand army, is he therefore qualified for a separate command here? If I thought you ignorant of his character, I would describe it more particularly, having had it in my power to make many observations on it. But you know it, DUER knows it, and Congress and General WASHINGTON are both well satisfied of his incapacity—and yet he commands; through indolence or false delicacy, the safety of one of the United States, and not the least important of them, is cruelly to be sacrificed. For Heaven's sake, rouse from your lethargy—change the command—take some steps for our security; before this reaches you, we shall be far advanced in February, and no step of any importance taken for our defence. If nothing is done, our State will be depopulated—the inhabitants within many miles of the river are already seeking more quiet dwellings. The lands will remain unsown, least the enemy should reap. I am fearful that all your expedition, should you exert yourself immediately upon the receipt of this, will still be too slow—but leave nothing unattempted. Let us, whatever happens, have the consolation of reflecting that we have neglected nothing that our love for our country suggested—and let the rectitude of our intentions give the lie to the artful or insidious attempts of our enemies." * * * *

EXTRACT OF A LETTER FROM ROBT. R. LIVINGSTON TO GEN. WASHINGTON, IN REPLY TO HIS LETTER OF MARCH 12, 1778.

"April 12, 1778.

"The object of the inquiry into the loss of the forts, are not so extensive as *the public censures; they* comprehend that of the ships, and the subsequent destruction of the country, which was most shamefully abandoned. I believe, however, that the articles as they stand will be sufficient to discover, *at the least*, the *incapacity* of General PUTNAM, which, though it may hurt our delicacy, I conceive *a sufficient ground for the removal of any officer*, upon whose abilities the lives of men and the freedom

I. The accomplished Captain GRAYDON (*Memoirs*, edit. Phila., 1846, page 179,) says: "Thinking so highly as I now do of the gentlemen of this country, (*New England*,) the recollection is painful, but the fact must not be dissembled: even the celebrated General PUTNAM, riding with a hanger belted across his brawny shoulders, over a waistcoat without sleeves, (his summer costume,) was deemed much fitter to head a band of sicklemen or ditchers, than musketeers. He might be brave, and had, certainly, an honest manliness about him; but it was thought, and perhaps with reason, that he was not what the times required."

II. In the well-known "*Political Alphabet*," of those times, the original manuscript of which is in the New York Historical Society's Library, I find, opposite the letter O, these lines,

"O—stands for cypher, and so let it be,
Grandmother *Putnam*, an emblem of thee."*

III. What the plain-spoken, honest and brave old Governor GEORGE CLINTON's opinion of PUTNAM was, can be

of the country may rest. In a republican government, no room is left for those prejudices and partialities which prevail in monarchies. There the honor of individuals is so interwoven in the constitution, as to become a part of it, and a support of the throne, which, in the opinion of the rulers, precedes the happiness of the people. Virtue is the basis of a republic; and that confines every man to the station in which he is most capable of rendering services to the community. Thus PUTNAM should, were he ten years younger, have my most hearty vote for a company of Grenadiers. Not having shaken off, with the old government, the prejudices we imbibed under it, we continue in military commands many *peace officers* and *dowager generals*, who bring the army into contempt, and render the most promising schemes abortive. If they must still continue in the military line, I would propose that they be sent to the *Board of War*, since it appears, from a late expedition, that some who are most inactive in the field, are most bold in the cabinet, and that those who let the season of action slip, are great in the projection of unseasonable expeditions. I am very happy in the new arrangements at Peekskill, and think we have, under the command of General McDOUGAL, a fine prospect of defending this most important post."

* In singular harmony with this sentiment was the opinion of GOUVERNEUR MORRIS, in a letter to General SCHUYLER, written soon after the loss of Forts Montgomery and Clinton: "Old PUTNAM is an *old woman*," he says, " and, therefore, much cannot be expected from him."—*History of the Republic*, by JOHN C. HAMILTON, 1, p. 323.

gathered from the following letter; and I believe that no honest man, at the present day, will dissent from his views, when the facts to which it refers shall have been brought to his notice:

"POUGHKEEPSIE, 28th December, 1777.

"DEAR SIR:—I was favored with the receipt of your letter of the 22d inst., some days since, and returned a short answer to it by the express who brought it; but as I have reason to believe you had left Peekskill before he got there, I conclude my letter has not been received. I have not a doubt but that there have been such unjust and dishonorable practices committed on the inhabitants as you mention, nor have I reason to believe they were without the knowledge of the commanding officer of the Department. Complaints have been exhibited *to him* of cattle, the property of the inhabitants of this State, living near Colonel ROBINSON's, being drove off by parties of the Continental troops, and sold at vendue in New England, without any account being rendered to the proprietors; and, if I am rightly informed, an officer, with a party, took sundry articles from ROBINSON's, sent them off and sold them, in like manner, in Connecticut, and has not accounted with the States for the proceeds. Of this I informed Gen. PUTNAM, and desired that an inquiry might be made into the conduct of the officer commanding the party, to which I was more particularly induced, as I found *he* had given an order on the Quarter-Master-General for the payment of the teams employed in carrying off those effects; but I have reason to believe he has had no regard to my request. Of this I am fully convinced, that the soldiery claim as lawful prize every thing they take within the enemy's lines, though the property of our best friends, and whatever is taken beyond our advanced posts, by a generous construction, comes within the above predicament. On this principle, the several articles taken at or near ROBINSON's were sold, because the enemy's shipping were then in the river near that place; and, on the same principle, indiscriminate plunder might have taken place on both sides of the river, as high up as the manor of Livingston. Little good can be expected of an army whose interest it is to suffer a country to be abandoned to the enemy, thereby to justify plundering the inhabitants. Perhaps, and I don't know that it would be uncharitable to suppose, that it is this trade that makes some people so very fond of little expeditions.

"I have long thought to ascertain these facts, and seek redress, not only for the parties immediately injured, but the public: but my time has been so fully employed of late about other matters, that I have been obliged to neglect it.

* * * * * * * *

"Your most obedient servant,
"GEO. CLINTON.
"Lieut. Col. ALEXANDER HAMILTON."

When it is borne in mind that General PUTNAM, at the period in question, was "the commanding officer of the Department;" that, as such, his proportion of every "*lawful prize*" was much larger than that which his subordinates received; that his head-quarters were at ROBINSON'S; that it is said, the remains of his wife have found a resting-place in the vault of that family; and that it was *his* great fondness for "little expeditions" which caused so much trouble, the crushing force of this letter will be duly appreciated, and ISRAEL PUTNAM's integrity receive its appropriate respect.

IV. It will be recollected that in October, 1777, General WASHINGTON dispatched his aide-de-camp, Lieutenant-Colonel HAMILTON, to General GATES, to procure reinforcements from the Northern army; that, on his way up the Hudson, HAMILTON directed General PUTNAM to send three brigades from his command for the same purpose; and that this order was disregarded. On his return from Albany, HAMILTON stopped at New Windsor a second time, when he wrote to General WASHINGTON in these very emphatic words: "I am pained beyond expression to inform your Excellency that on my arrival here, I find every thing has been neglected and deranged by General PUTNAM, and that the two brigades, POOR's and LEARNED's, still remain here

and on the other side of the river, at Fishkill. Colonel WARNER's militia, I am told, have been drawn to Peekskill, to aid in an expedition against New York, which it seems is, at this time, the hobby-horse with General PUTNAM. Not the least attention has been paid to my order, in your name, for a detachment of one thousand men from the troops hitherto stationed at this post. Every thing is sacrificed to the whim of taking New York."* * * *
"I wish General PUTNAM was recalled from the command of this post, and Governor CLINTON would accept it—the blunders and caprices of the former are endless. Believe me, sir, nobody can be more impressed with the importance of forwarding the reinforcements coming to you with all speed, nor could any body have endeavored to promote it more than I have done; but the *ignorance* of some, and the *design* of others, have been almost insuperable obstacles." (*Hamilton's Letter to General Washington, Nov. 10th,* 1777.) Again, two days later, he writes, "I must do him (General POOR) the justice to say he appears solicitous to join you, and that I believe the past delay is not owing to any fault of his, but is wholly chargeable on General PUTNAM. Indeed, sir, I owe it to the service to say, that every part of *this gentleman's* conduct is marked with blunder and negligence, and gives general disgust." (*Lieut-Col. Hamilton's Letter to Gen. Washington,* Nov. 12, 1777.) To these letters General WASHINGTON gave this answer (*Letter to Lieut-Col. Hamilton,* Nov. 15, 1777) : "I approve entirely of all the steps you have taken, and have only to wish that the exertions of those you have had to deal with, had kept pace with your zeal and good intentions."†

---

* The force of Gov. GEORGE CLINTON's remark on "*little expeditions*" (*vide* p. 159) will be seen from this paragraph.

† The curious will find interesting matter connected with this subject in "*The History of the Republic,*" by JOHN C. HAMILTON, vol. 1, pp. 358–361.

By a reference to ROBERT R. LIVINGSTON's letter to General WASHINGTON, which I cited in my last letter, and a comparison with this, it will be seen that, in their allusion to the sentiments of the people, and of the army then posted in the Highlands, there is a wonderful agreement in their language, respecting the popular opinion concerning PUTNAM's character and ability.

V. "*Selah*" refers with great satisfaction to a complimentary letter which General JOSEPH REED wrote to PUTNAM; and from that he proves, to his own satisfaction, that PUTNAM must have enjoyed the confidence and respect of the former officer. I have before me a pamphlet, written by General REED, entitled "*Remarks on a late publication in the Independent Gazette; with a short address to the People of Pennsylvania on the many libels and slanders which have lately appeared against the author*, Phila., 1783," in which the matter is fully discussed. These are his words: "At this juncture the plan of attack on the Hessians at Trenton was completed, and preparations made for carrying it into effect, on the morning of the 26th of December, when it was supposed that the festivities of the preceding day would make surprise more easy, and conquest more certain. As soon as it was fully determined, General WASHINGTON wrote me the letter of the 23d of December, which will certainly convey, to every unprejudiced mind, a clear idea of the unbounded confidence reposed in my fidelity at so critical a period, when the fate of America hung in most critical and awful suspense. The letter, of course, I communicated to General CADWALLADER; and, as Colonel GRIFFEN had retired, and General WASHINGTON expressed such earnest desires that a diversion should be made for Count DONOP, we concluded to engage General PUTNAM, then in Philadelphia, to attempt it, by crossing at Cooper's Ferry, with the troops then daily coming in. A difficulty then presented—how we should make the communication to General PUTNAM, without entrusting this important secret farther than *prudence* and the General's strong injunctions would warrant. After various suggestions, General CADWALLADER, with some apologies, proposed that I should go and enforce it with personal influence. I accordingly set out in the evening, and reached Philadelphia at midnight; upon conference with General PUTNAM, he represented the state of the militia, the general confusion which prevailed, his apprehensions of an insurrection in the city in his absence, and many other circumstances, as convinced me no assistance could be derived from him."

When it is borne in mind, that in these, the very darkest days of the Revolutionary war, when every nerve was strained, and every possible resource called into requisition to facilitate the movements and insure the success of the commander-in-chief, in his proposed assault on Colonel RAHL, at Trenton, it was not considered "*prudent*," or warranted by "the General's strong injunctions," to "entrust this important secret" to General PUTNAM, (even when the effect of that want of confidence would be the loss of General PUTNAM's coöperation, with that of the garrison of Philadelphia, and of "the troops then daily coming in,") it will be seen, more distinctly than from any words of mine, what were the peculiar opinions, respecting General PUTNAM's character and fidelity to his country, which Generals JOHN CADWALLADER, JOSEPH REED, and GEORGE WASHINGTON, entertained in December, 1776; and if "*Selah*" and his faithful squire are content with them, neither I nor "the mass of the people of Connecticut" have any cause of complaint.

VI. My zealous opponents, hard pushed for material, have also pressed into their service a letter of the illustrious WASHINGTON, written after the cessation of hostilities, when his half-pay was the subject of anxiety in Gen. PUTNAM's mind. It would have been more candid, I think, if the letter of the Commander-in-chief to the President of Congress, respecting the discontent in the army on the occasion of PUTNAM's appointment to the office of Major-General, had been cited. It is dated at "Cambridge, July 4th, 1775," and can be seen, at length, in *Dr. Sparks' Writings of Washington*, III., pp. 22, 23. There is a letter from General WASHINGTON, dated "Valley Forge, March 6, 1778," which, also, "*Selah*" could have studied profitably. One clause of that letter, referring to the Rhode Island expedition, reads thus: "They also know, with more certainty than I do, what will be the determination of Congress respecting General PUTNAM, and, of course, whether the appointment of him to such a command as that at Rhode Island, would fall within their views: it being incumbent on me to observe, that with such materials as I am furnished, the work must go on—whether well or ill is another matter. If, therefore, he and others are not laid aside, they must be placed where they can least injure the service." There is information, also, on this subject, in that powerfully-written letter of General WASHINGTON to President JOHN JAY, dated "Head-quarters, Middlebrook, April 14, 1779," in which, after discussing the machinations of General GATES, he says, "The plan of operations for the campaign being determined, a commanding officer was to be appointed for the Indian expedition. This command, according to all present appearances, will probably be of the second, if not the first importance for the campaign.

The officer conducting it has a flattering prospect of acquiring more credit, than can be expected by any other, this year; and he has the best reason to hope for success. General LEE, from his situation, was out of the question; General SCHUYLER (who, by the way, would have been most agreeable to me,) was so uncertain of continuing in the army, that I could not appoint him; General PUTNAM I need not mention. I, therefore, made the offer of it, for the appointment could not longer be delayed, to General GATES," &c. Probably General WASHINGTON, like some persons at the present day, had never seen the evidence of PUTNAM's exploits among the Indians, which "*Selah*" and his squire have spoken of; and it is really a great pity that the HUMPHREYS, the SWETTS, the CUTTERS, the DEMINGS, and the "*Selahs*" of more modern times, had not then existed to enlighten the Virginia gentleman who was then at the head of the army, concerning the wonderful abilities, as a scout and woodsman, which General PUTNAM possessed. Had the General supposed that General PUTNAM was worthy of his notice, he would at least have "mentioned him," in connection with the command; or, had he supposed that he possessed any merit as a "scout"—of which the living witnesses were in his camp—he would have honored him with the command, especially since General SULLIVAN was vested with it, from necessity. The truth is, General WASHINGTON was, himself, a "woodsman," and knew what was the exact extent of PUTNAM's qualifications for the command. He knew that making gardens, and mending roads, and cutting firewood had been the chief employments of the hero of the fox's hole, during the preceding war with France; and now, when active service, good judgment, undoubted bravery, and the finest military abilities were required, he knew, also, that PUTNAM was not qualified for the post, and he did "not mention" him. The correspondence between ROBERT R. LIVINGSTON and General WASHINGTON, early in 1778, from which extracts were given in my last, will have conveyed to "*Selah*," by this time, probably, what was General WASHINGTON's opinion of PUTNAM at that time; while his answer to Lieutenant Colonel HAMILTON's letter (*Letter to Hamilton*, Nov. 15, 1777,) will show what his opinion of "*Selah's*" hero was at the close of the preceding year.

Were such authorities necessary for my purpose, I could add many others to those which I have already cited, from officers of the American army; and we are not entirely without evidence that the British officers entertained similar views. Indeed, it is well known that the correspondence of General ROBERTSON and Major ANDRE, which led to the open desertion of one party and the death of another, was not confined exclusively to BENEDICT ARNOLD.* The enemy, by long continued correspondence, such as ROBERT R. LIVINGSTON protested against in January, 1778, had become as well acquainted with PUTNAM's failings as with ARNOLD's poverty;† and when a deed of darker hue than usual was projected, the cupidity of the one and the necessities of the other were the instrumentalities whose

---

* The evidence is before me, which clearly proves the complicity of Gen. PUTNAM, with ARNOLD, in the West Point Treason, for which Major ANDRE was hung and Gen. ARNOLD became an exile and an outlaw.

† Gen. GAGE, the Royal Governor of Massachusetts, in the earlier days of the Revolution, was made acquainted, directly, with PUTNAM's failings; and was, afterwards, censured for not profiting from that knowledge. At a subsequent date, a letter from New York, published in "*The Middlesex Journal*," a London paper, on the twenty-first of December, 1776, says: "*He* (PUTNAM) *never was a favorer of American Independency;*" and the "old friend of General PUTNAM's," who wrote this letter, although he was *then in New York*, was, doubtless, well informed concerning his views.

co-operation, within the American lines, were sought by ANDRE and his superiors. It may serve to amuse "*Selah*" and his man Friday, at some future time, however; and I will close the record, temporarily, without troubling your readers on this subject at the present time.*

The question respecting the commandant on Breed's Hill, Mr. Editor, is by no means a new one; and "*Selah*" is not the first of PUTNAM's friends who has mooted it. Early in the day, on the 17th of June, 1775, a friend of PUTNAM— one THOMAS GAGE, a Major-General in the King's service —inquired from a royalist who stood at his side, in the town of Boston, "Who is the person who appears to command?"† and from that day to the present—from General GAGE to "*Selah*"—the same question has been asked, and as often answered. Councillor WILLARD, recognizing, in Colonel PRESCOTT, his own brother-in-law, answered GAGE; Mr. FROTHINGHAM has responded to Colonel SWETT; and upon me, in the midst of the pressing cares of business, has devolved the duty of making the last answer, to your correspondent "*Selah*."

With my sincere thanks to yourself, and to your readers, for the patience with which you and they have endured this prolonged discussion, I remain, as ever,

Sincerely yours,

HENRY B. DAWSON.

P. S.—*July 29th*. Since the date of this letter, I have been favored, by my courteous opponent, with copies of three efforts, auxiliary to his own, which have found their

---

* My friend, "*Selah*," having failed to raise the curtain, the discussion of this topic must, necessarily, rest until another opportunity shall have been offered.

† Vide FROTHINGHAM's *Siege of Boston*, p. 126.

way into the press of Hartford—a poem, by Mrs. SIGOURNEY; a series of resolutions, denunciatory of me, and laudatory of PUTNAM and "*Selah,*" by the "Putnam Phalanx," of Hartford; and a series of resolutions, similar to the last, by the Legislature of Connecticut. If I may be allowed to judge, from these signs, I might suppose that Connecticut is becoming somewhat excited. It is from just such agitations as this, however, that the truth is developed; and while my opponents continue to stir up the matter, falsehood will lose ground.

The poem is all which any one can make on such an empty subject; and if it is but "sounding brass," the fault is in the subject, not in Mrs. SIGOURNEY.

The "Phalanx," like good neighbors, have held up the weary hands of their young townsman, and, by their sympathy, have cheered the heart of their associate.* They have done well; and they, too, should engross their pro-

---

* The following is a copy of the preamble and resolutions referred to, taken from "*The Hartford Daily Post,*" of Saturday, May 14, 1859:

"PUTNAM PHALANX.

"At a regular meeting of the PUTNAM PHALANX, holden at their Armory, last evening, the following resolutions were offered by Mr. E. B. STRONG, Quarter-master of the battalion, which were unanimously adopted, and ordered to be published in each of the daily papers.

"*Whereas,* Certain correspondence having recently taken place in "*The Hartford Daily Post,*" between HENRY B. DAWSON and "*Selah,*" affecting the fair fame and military reputation of one whose memory we fondly cherish; therefore,

"*Resolved,* That the hearty thanks of the PUTNAM PHALANX, of Hartford, Conn., are hereby tendered to our fellow-citizen and soldier, "*Selah,*" (A. CLIFFORD GRISWOLD, Esq.,) for the able and unanswerable vindication he has made, through the "*Daily Post,*" of the immortal name that adorns their military association.

"*Resolved,* That the unpatriotic and prejudiced author of the "*Battles of the United States by Sea and Land,*" (HENRY B. DAWSON,) deserves no welcome consideration from the hands of that free people to whose welfare Major-General ISRAEL PUTNAM devoted his courage, his ardor, and his inflexible love of liberty!

(Attest) "J. M. SEXTON, *Sec'y.*"

ceedings, on this subject, either in the ancient "town records" of Pomfret, where "*Selah*" says the record of PUTNAM's birth in Connecticut can be seen;* or, what is better, probably, in the archives of "The Historical Society of Connecticut."†

The General Assembly of Connecticut has also decreed that that State has furnished "not only the hero, but the commander" at Bunker's Hill.‡ Why did not that sage

---

* Vide "*Selah's*" first letter.

† Vide the Resolutions of the Legislature of Connecticut, referred to in the next note.

‡ It appears from *marked* papers which were sent to me, that the Hon. HENRY C. DEMING, a member of the House, had delivered a "Lecture" on "*The Life and Services of Major-General* ISRAEL PUTNAM," before the members of the Legislature of Connecticut; and, soon afterwards, the two Houses of that body passed resolutions approving the sentiments which the lecturer had expressed, passing judgment on the manner in which he had handled his subject, and determining the questions which were involved in the then pending discussion between "*Selah*" and his opponent. The following abstract of the proceedings, taken from the Legislative reports in "*The Hartford Daily Post*," of June 17, 1859—a reminiscence of Bunker's Hill—will convey to the reader the spirit of the House, as well as the sentiments of the lecturer.

"CONNECTICUT LEGISLATURE.

"SENATE.

"THURSDAY, June 16.

* * * * * * * *

"Resolution of thanks to Hon. HENRY C. DEMING for his address on the Life and Services of General PUTNAM. Passed unanimously."

"HOUSE.

"THURSDAY, June 16.

* * * * * * * *

"Mr. BRANDAGEE offered the following resolutions:

"*Resolved*, That the unanimous thanks of this Assembly are due, and are hereby tendered to the HON. HENRY C. DEMING, of Hartford, for his very eloquent lecture, delivered, at the request of the two Houses, on the Life and Services of General ISRAEL PUTNAM; and especially for his *masterly* and *conclusive* vindication of the claim of Connecticut to have furnished to the cause of Liberty on Bunker's Hill, not only the *hero*, but the COMMANDANT.

"*Resolved*, That the clerks of the respective Houses be instructed to procure copies of this resolve, to be appropriately executed upon parchment, at the expense of the State, one of which shall be furnished to Mr. DEMING, and the other deposited in the State Historical Society; and that this resolution be entered at length in the journals of the two houses respectively.

assembly, in its wisdom, also enact that Connecticut has also furnished the historian who has discovered it, and the Legislature which has given it the sanction of a legal enactment? The National Assembly of France enacted, in due form, the assertion that there is no God; the Assembly of Connecticut, emulous of Gallic reputation, has, with equal gravity, enacted that a Massachusetts man, named PUTNAM, was "not only the hero, but the commander on Bunker's Hill"—a question which is beyond the scope of the powers of that Body; and one which is not, and will not be affected by all the resolutions which may be adopted concerning it, from this day to the end of time.

H. B. D.

Mr. BRANDAGEE said: Any gentleman who was in attendance upon the lecture referred to in the resolution, could speak on this subject as well as he could. But he never attended a lecture on any subject—scientific, philosophical or historical—in which he had been more completely interested, or in which the case was more ably handled, than in this instance. And he believed that Connecticut was interested to have a record of this proceeding upon the pages of the journals of the Legislature.

Mr. HALSEY remarked that the oration was a triumphant vindication of the claims of General PUTNAM and of Connecticut, and the resolution expressed his opinion precisely. He felt sure that all would give their commendation in favor of the *Orator* and in commemoration of the HERO.

The resolution passed *nem. con.*

Mr. DEMING begged leave to trespass upon strict parliamentary rules so far as to express his thanks for the compliment contained in this resolution, and he offered his thanks to the gentleman who offered the resolution (Mr. BRANDAGEE) and the gentleman who supported it (Mr. HALSEY). It was time that there should be some vindication of the fame of PUTNAM and the honor of Connecticut. Since the lecture last evening he had received renewed evidence of the truth of the claim that Gen. PUTNAM commanded at the battle of Bunker's Hill. He had met with men from Windham County who had received traditional evidence that in that battle PUTNAM was the chief in command. And these persons did not know that this fact was doubted. Surely, they have not read the works of BANCROFT, or IRVING, or FROTHINGHAM, or the reports in the papers of the meeting in Boston after the death of PRESCOTT, when it was claimed that his father was the commander at that battle. And many did not know that PRESCOTT's claim was doubted. But he had searched all the authorities, and could not entertain a doubt of the valid claim that Connecticut holds in this case. To the end of his life did PUTNAM claim this honor, and when almost *in articulo mortis* he bequeathed the claim to his son. To the extent that I have assisted in vindicating this claim I rejoice, and I will not say how flattered I feel as regards the action of the House. [Spontaneous and hearty applause.]"

www.ingramcontent.com/pod-product-compliance
Lightning Source LLC
Chambersburg PA
CBHW030244170426
43202CB00009B/624